Creating a Data-Driven Enterprise with DataOps
Insights from Facebook, Uber, LinkedIn, Twitter, and eBay

Ashish Thusoo and Joydeep Sen Sarma

Beijing · Boston · Farnham · Sebastopol · Tokyo

Creating a Data-Driven Enterprise with DataOps

by Ashish Thusoo and Joydeep Sen Sarma

Copyright © 2017 O'Reilly Media, Inc. All rights reserved.

Printed in the United States of America.

Published by O'Reilly Media, Inc., 1005 Gravenstein Highway North, Sebastopol, CA 95472.

O'Reilly books may be purchased for educational, business, or sales promotional use. Online editions are also available for most titles (*http://oreilly.com/safari*). For more information, contact our corporate/institutional sales department: 800-998-9938 or *corporate@oreilly.com*.

Editor: Nicole Tache
Production Editor: Kristen Brown
Copyeditor: Octal Publishing, Inc.
Interior Designer: David Futato
Cover Designer: Karen Montgomery
Illustrator: Rebecca Demarest

April 2017:   First Edition

Revision History for the First Edition
2017-04-24:   First Release

978-1-491-97781-1

[LSI]

Table of Contents

Part II. Case Studies

Acknowledgments

This book is an attempt to capture what we have learned building teams, systems, and processes in our constant pursuit of a data-driven approach for the companies that we have worked for, as well as companies that are clients of Qubole today. To capture the essence of those learnings has taken effort and support from a number of people.

We cannot express enough thanks to David Hsieh for noticing the prescient need for a book on this topic and then constantly encouraging us to put our learnings to paper. We are also thankful to him for creating the maturity model for big data based on the patterns of our learnings about the adoption cycle of big data in the enterprise. At all the steps of the creation of this book, David has been a great sounding board and has given timely and useful advice. Thanks are also equally due to Karyn Scott for managing everything and anything related to the book, from coordinating the logistics with O'Reilly, to working behind the scenes with the Qubole team to polish the diagrams and presentations. She has constantly pushed to strive for timely delivery of the manuscript, which at times was understandably frustrating given that both of us were working on this while building out Qubole. Thanks are also due to Mauro Calvi and Dharmesh Desai for capturing some of the discussions in easy-to-digest pictorial representations.

We also want to thank the entire production team at O'Reilly, starting with Nicole Tache who edited a number of versions of the manuscript to ensure that not just the content but also our voice was well represented. We are grateful for her flexibility in the production process so that we could get the content right. Also at O'Reilly, we want to thank Alice LaPlante for diligently capturing our interviews on the subject and for helping build the content based on those interviews.

This book also tries to look for patterns that are common in enterprises that have achieved the "nirvana" of being data-driven. In that aspect, the contributions of Debashis Saha (eBay), Karthik Ramasamy (Twitter), Shrikanth Shankar (LinkedIn), and Zheng Shao (Uber) are some of the most valuable to the book as well as to our collective knowledge. All of these folks are great practitioners of the art and science of making their companies data-driven, and we are very thankful to them for sharing their learnings and experiences, and in the process making this book all the more insightful.

Last but not least, thanks to our families for putting up with us while we worked on this book. Without their constant encouragement and support, this effort would not have been possible.

Foundations of a Data-Driven Enterprise

This book is divided into two parts. In Part I, we discuss the theoretical and practical foundations for building a self-service, data-driven company.

In Chapter 1, we explain why data-driven companies are more successful and profitable than companies that do not center their decision-making on data. We also define what DataOps is and explain why moving to a self-service infrastructure is so critical.

In Chapter 2, we trace the history of data over the past three decades and how analytics has evolved accordingly. We then introduce the Qubole Self-Service Maturity Model to show how companies progress from a relatively simple state to a mature state that makes data ubiquitous to all employees through self-service.

In Chapter 3, we discuss the important distinctions between data warehouses and data lakes, and why, at least for now, you need to have both to effectively manage big data.

In Chapter 4, we define what a data-driven company is and how to successfully build, support, and evolve one.

In Chapter 5, we explore the need for a complete, integrated, and self-service data infrastructure, and the personas and tools that are required to support this.

In Chapter 6, we talk about how the cloud makes building a self-service infrastructure much easier and more cost effective. We explore the five capabilities of cloud to show why it makes the perfect enabler for a self-service culture.

In Chapter 7, we define metadata, and explain why it is essential for a successful self-service, data-driven operation.

In Chapter 8, we reveal the results of a Qubole survey that show the current state of maturity of global organizations today.

CHAPTER 1

Introduction

The Journey Begins

My journey with big data began at Oracle, led me to Facebook, and, finally, to founding Qubole. It's been an exciting and informative ride, full of learnings and epiphanies. But two early "ah-ha's" in particular stand out. They both occurred at Facebook. One was that users were eager to get their hands on data directly, without going through the data engineers in the data team. The second was how powerful data could be in the hands of the people.

I joined Facebook in August 2007 as part of the data team. It was a new group, set up in the traditional way for that time. The data infrastructure team supported a small group of data professionals who were called upon whenever anyone needed to access or analyze data located in a traditional data warehouse. As was typical in those days, anyone in the company who wanted to get data beyond some small and curated summaries stored in the data warehouse had to come to the data team and make a request. Our data team was excellent, but it could only work so fast: it was a clear bottleneck.

I was delighted to find a former classmate from my undergraduate days at the Indian Institute of Technology already at Facebook. Joydeep Sen Sarma had been hired just a month previously. Our team's charter was simple: to make Facebook's rich trove of data more available.

Our initial challenge was that we had a nonscalable infrastructure that had hit its limits. So, our first step was to experiment with

Hadoop. Joydeep created the first Hadoop cluster at Facebook and the first set of jobs, populating the first datasets to be consumed by other engineers—application logs collected using Scribe and application data stored in MySQL.

But Hadoop wasn't (and still isn't) particularly user friendly, even for engineers. Gartner found that even today—due to how difficult it is to find people with adequate Hadoop skills—more than half of businesses (54 percent) have no plans to invest in it.[1] It was, and is, a challenging environment. We found that the productivity of our engineers suffered. The bottleneck of data requests persisted (see Figure 1-1).

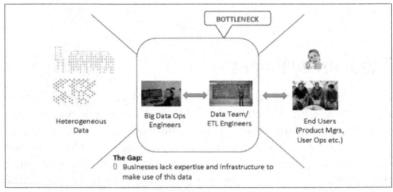

Figure 1-1. Human bottlenecks (source: Qubole)

SQL, on the other hand, was widely used by both engineers and analysts, and was powerful enough for most analytics requirements. So Joydeep and I decided to make the programmability of Hadoop available to everyone. Our idea: to create a SQL-based declarative language that would allow engineers to plug in their own scripts and programs when SQL wasn't adequate. In addition, it was built to store all of the metadata about Hadoop-based datasets in one place. This latter feature was important because it turned out indispensable for creating the data-driven company that Facebook subsequently became.

---

1 *http://www.gartner.com/newsroom/id/3051717*

That language, of course, was Hive, and the rest is history. Still, the idea was very new to us. We had no idea whether it would succeed. But it did. The data team immediately became more productive. The bottleneck eased. But then something happened that surprised us.

In January of 2008, when we released the first version of Hive internally at Facebook, a rush of employees—data scientists and engineers—grabbed the interfaces for themselves. They began to access the data they needed directly. They didn't bother to request help from the data team. With Hive, we had inadvertently brought the power of big data to the people. We immediately saw tremendous opportunities in completely democratizing data. That was our first "ah-ha!"

One of the things driving employees to Hive was that at that same time (January 2008) Facebook released its Ad product.

Over the course of the next six months, a number of employees began to use the system heavily. Although the initial use case for Hive and Hadoop centered around summarizing and analyzing clickstream data for the launch of the Facebook Ad program, Hive quickly began to be used by product teams and data scientists for a number of other projects. In addition, we first talked about Hive at the first Hadoop summit, and immediately realized the tremendous potential beyond just what Facebook was doing with it.

With this, we had our second "ah-ha"—that by making data more universally accessible within the company, we could actually disrupt our entire industry. Data in the hands of the people was that powerful. As an aside, some time later we saw another example of what happens when you make data universally available.

Facebook used to have "hackathons," where everyone in the company stayed up all night, ordered pizza and beer, and coded into the wee hours with the goal of coming up with something interesting. One intern—Paul Butler—came up with a spectacular idea. He performed analyses using Hadoop and Hive and mapped out how Facebook users were interacting with each other all over the world. By drawing the interactions between people and their locations, he developed a global map of Facebook's reach. Astonishingly, it mapped out all continents and even some individual countries.

In Paul's own words:

> When I shared the image with others within Facebook, it resonated with many people. It's not just a pretty picture, it's a reaffirmation of the impact we have in connecting people, even across oceans and borders.

To me, this was nothing short of amazing. By using data, this intern came up with an incredibly creative idea, incredibly quickly. It could never have happened in the old world when a data team was needed to fulfill all requests for data.

Data was clearly too important to be left behind lock and key, accessible only by data engineers. We were on our way to turning Facebook into a data-driven company.

The Emergence of the Data-Driven Organization

84 percent of executives surveyed said they believe that "most to all" of their employees should use data analysis to help them perform their job duties.

Let's discuss why data is important, and what a data-driven organization is. First and foremost, a data-driven organization is one that understands the importance of data. It possesses a culture of using data to make all business decisions. Note the word *all*. In a data-driven organization, no one comes to a meeting armed only with hunches or intuition. The person with the superior title or largest salary doesn't win the discussion. Facts do. Numbers. Quantitative analyses. Stuff backed up by data.

Why become a data-driven company? Because it pays off. The MIT Center for Digital Business asked 330 companies about their data analytics and business decision-making processes. It found that the more companies characterized themselves as data-driven, the better they performed on objective measures of financial and operational success.[2]

Specifically, companies in the top third of their industries when it came to making data-driven decisions were, on average, five percent more productive and six percent more profitable than their compet-

---

2 *https://hbr.org/2012/10/big-data-the-management-revolution*

itors. This performance difference remained even after accounting for labor, capital, purchased services, and traditional IT investments. It was also statistically significant and reflected in increased stock market prices that could be objectively measured.

Another survey, by The Economist Intelligence Unit, showed a clear connection between how a company uses data, and its financial success. Only 11 percent of companies said that their organization makes "substantially" better use of data than their peers. Yet more than a third of this group fell into the category of "top performing companies."[3] The reverse also indicates the relationship between data and financial success. Of the 17 percent of companies that said they "lagged" their peers in taking advantage of data, not one was a top-performing business.

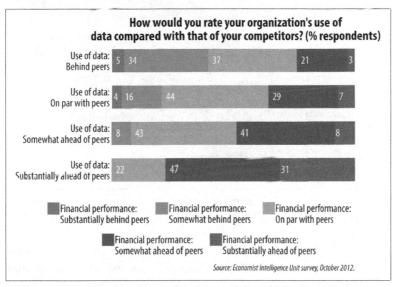

Figure 1-2. Rating an organization's use of data (data from Economist Intelligence Unit survey, October 2012)

Another Economist Intelligence Unit survey found that 70 percent of senior business executives said analyzing data for sales and marketing decisions is already "very" or "extremely important" to their

---

3 https://www.tableau.com/sites/default/files/whitepapers/tableau_datacul ture_130219.pdf

company's competitive advantage. A full 89 percent of respondents expect this to be the case within two years.[4]

According to the aforementioned MIT report, 50 percent of "above-average" performing businesses said they had achieved a data-driven company by the promotion of data sharing. More than half (57 percent) said that a data-driven company was driven by top-down mandates from the highest level. And an eye-opening 84 percent of executives surveyed said they believe that "most to all" of their employees should use data analysis to help them perform their job duties, not just IT workers or data scientists and analysts.[5]

Figure 1-3. Successful strategies for promoting a data-driven culture (data from Economist Intelligence Unit survey, October 2012)

But how do you become a data-driven company? That is something this book will address in later chapters. But according to a *Harvard Business Review* article written by McKinsey executives, being a data-driven company requires simultaneously undertaking three interdependent initiatives:[6]

---

4 http://www.zsassociates.com/publications/articles/Broken-links-Why-analytics-investments-have-yet-to-pay-off.aspx

5 http://www.contegix.com/the-importance-of-a-data-driven-company-culture/

6 https://hbr.org/2012/10/making-advanced-analytics-work-for-you

Identify, combine, and manage multiple sources of data
You might already have all the data you need. Or you might need to be creative to find other sources for it. Either way, you need to eliminate silos of data while constantly seeking out new sources to inform your decision-making. And it's critical to remember that when mining data for insights, demanding data from different and independent sources leads to much better decisions. Today, both the sources and the amount of data you can collect has increased by orders of magnitude. It's a connected world, given all the transactions, interactions, and, increasingly, sensors that are generating data. And the fact is, if you combine multiple independent sources, you get better insight. The companies that do this are in much better shape, financially and operationally.

Build advanced analytics models for predicting and optimizing outcomes
The most effective approach is to identify a business opportunity and determine how the model can achieve it. In other words, you don't start with the data—at least at first—but with a problem.

Transform the organization and culture of the company so that data actually produces better business decisions
Many big data initiatives fail because they aren't in sync with a company's day-to-day processes and decision-making habits. Data professionals must understand what decisions their business users make, and give users the tools they need to make those decisions. (More on this in Chapter 5.)

So, why are we hearing about the failure of so many big data initiatives? One PricewaterhouseCoopers study found that only four percent of companies with big data initiatives consider them successful. Almost half (43 percent) of companies "obtain little tangible benefit from their information," and 23 percent "derive no benefit whatsoever."[7] Sobering statistics.

It turns out that despite the benefits of a data-driven culture, creating one can be difficult. It requires a major shift in the thinking and

---

7 *http://www.cio.com/article/3003538/big-data/study-reveals-that-most-companies-are-failing-at-big-data.html*

business practices of all employees at an organization. Any bottlenecks between the employees who need data and the keepers of data must be completely eliminated. This is probably why only two percent of companies in the MIT report believe that attempts to transform their companies using data have had a "broad, positive impact."[8]

Indeed, one of the reasons that we were so quickly able to move to a data-driven environment at Facebook was the company culture. It is very empowering, and everyone is encouraged to innovate when seeking ways to do their jobs better. As Joydeep and I began building Hive, and as it became popular, we transitioned to being a new kind of company. It was actually easy for us, *because* of the culture. We talk more about that in Chapter 3.

Moving to Self-Service Data Access

After we released Hive, the genie was out of the bottle. The company was on fire. Everyone wanted to run their own queries and analyses on Facebook data.

In just six months, we had fulfilled our initial charter, to make data more easily available to the data team. By March 2008, we were given the official mandate to make data accessible to everyone in the company. Suddenly, we had a new problem: keeping the infrastructure up and available, and scaling it to meet the demands of hundreds of employees (which would over the next few years become thousands). So, making sure everyone had their fair share of the company's data infrastructure quickly became our number-one challenge.

That's when we realized that *data delayed is data denied*. Opportunities slip by quickly. Not being able to leap immediately onto a trend and ride it to business success could hurt the company directly.

We had the first steps to self-service data *access*. Now we needed an infrastructure that could support self-service access at scale. Self-service data *infrastructure*. Instead of simply building infrastructure for the data team, we had to think about how to build infrastructure that could fairly share the resources across different teams, and

---

8 *http://www.zsassociates.com/publications/articles/Broken-links-Why-analytics-investments-have-yet-to-pay-off.aspx*

could do so in a way that was controlled and easily auditable. We also had to make sure that this infrastructure could be built incrementally so that we could add capacity as dictated by the demands of the users.

As Figure 1-4 illustrates, moving from manual infrastructure provisioning processes—which creates the same bottlenecks that occurred with the old model of data access—to a self-service one gives employees a much faster response to their data-access needs at a much lower operating cost. Think about it: just as you had the data team positioned between the employees and the data, now you had the same wall between employees and infrastructure. Having theoretical access to data did employees no good when they had to go to the data team to request infrastructure resources every time they wanted to query the data.

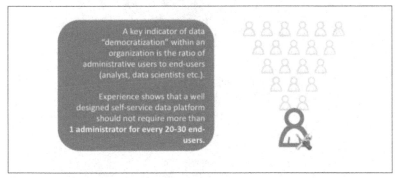

Figure 1-4. User-to-admin ratio

The absence of such capabilities in the data infrastructure caused delays. And it hurt the business. Employees often needed fast iterations on queries to make their creative ideas come to fruition. All too often, a great idea is a fast idea: it must be seized in a moment.

An infrastructure that does not support fair sharing also creates friction between prototype projects and production projects. Prototype stage projects need agility and flexibility. On the other hand, production projects need stability and predictability. A common infrastructure must also support these two diametrically opposite requirements. This single fact was one of the biggest challenges of coming up with mechanisms to promote a shared infrastructure that could support both ad hoc (prototyping or data exploration) self-service data access and production self-service data access.

Giving data access to everyone—even those who had no data training—was our goal. An additional aspect of the infrastructure to support self-service access to data is how the tools with which they are familiar integrate with the infrastructure. An employee's tools need to talk directly to the compute grid. If access to infrastructure is controlled by a specialized central team, you're effectively going back to your old model (Figure 1-5).

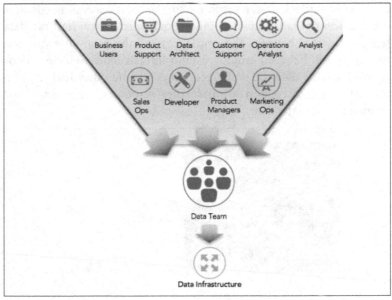

Figure 1-5. Reality of data access for a typical enterprise (source: Qubole)

The lesson learned: to truly democratize data, you need to transform both data access tools *and* infrastructure provisioning to a self-service model.

But this isn't just a matter of putting the right technology in place. Your company also needs to make a massive cultural shift. Collaboration must exist between data engineers, scientists, and analysts. You need to adopt the kind of culture that allows your employees to iterate rapidly when refining their data-driven ideas.

You need to create a *DataOps culture.*

The Emergence of DataOps

Once upon a time, corporate developers and IT operations professionals worked separately, in heavily armored silos. Developers wrote application code and "threw it over the wall" to the operations team, who then were responsible for making sure the applications worked when users actually had them in their hands. This was never an optimal way to work. But it soon became impossible as businesses began developing web apps. In the fast-paced digital world, they needed to roll out fresh code and updates to production rapidly. And it had to work. Unfortunately, it often didn't. So, organizations are now embracing a set of best practices known as *DevOps* that improve coordination between developers and the operations team.

DevOps is the practice of combining software engineering, quality assurance (QA), and operations into a single, agile organization. The practice is changing the way applications—particularly web apps—are developed and deployed within businesses.

Now a similar model, called DataOps, is changing the way data is consumed.

Here's Gartner's definition of DataOps:

> [A] hub for collecting and distributing data, with a mandate to provide controlled access to systems of record for customer and marketing performance data, while protecting privacy, usage restrictions, and data integrity.[9]

That mostly covers it. However, I prefer a slightly different, perhaps more pragmatic, hands-on definition:

> DataOps is a new way of managing data that promotes communication between, and integration of, formerly siloed data, teams, and systems. It takes advantage of process change, organizational realignment, and technology to facilitate relationships between everyone who handles data: developers, data engineers, data scientists, analysts, and business users. DataOps closely connects the people who collect and prepare the data, those who analyze the data, and those who put the findings from those analyses to good business use.

---

9 *http://www.gartner.com/it-glossary/data-ops/*

Figure 1-6 summarizes the aspirations for a data-driven enterprise—
one that follows the DataOps model. At the core of the data-driven
enterprise are executive support, a centralized data infrastructure,
and democratized data access. In this model, data is processed, analyzed for insights, and reused.

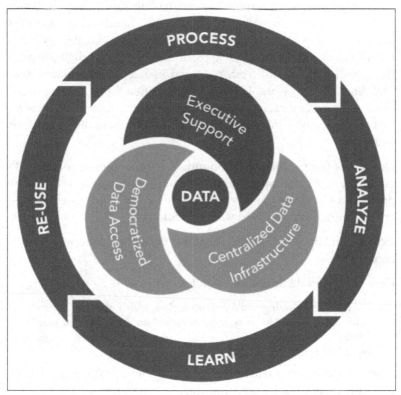

*Figure 1-6. The aspirations for a data-driven enterprise (source:
Qubole)*

Two trends are creating the need for DataOps:

The need for more agility with data
> Businesses today run at a very fast pace, so if data is not moving
> at the same pace, it is dropped from the decision-making pro-
> cess. This is similar to how the agility in creating web apps led
> to the creation of the DevOps culture. The same agility is now
> also needed on the data side.

Data becoming more mainstream

This ties back to the fact that in today's world there is a proliferation of data sources because of all the advancements in collection: new apps, sensors on the Internet of Things (IoT), and social media. There's also the increasing realization that data can be a competitive advantage. As data has become mainstream, the need to democratize it and make it accessible is felt very strongly within businesses today. In light of these trends, data teams are getting pressure from all sides.

In effect, data teams are having the same problem that application developers once had. Instead of developers writing code, we now have data scientists designing analytic models for extracting actionable insights from large volumes of data. But there's the problem: no matter how clever and innovative those data scientists are, they don't help the business if they can't get hold of the data or can't put the results of their models into the hands of decision-makers.

DataOps has therefore become a critical discipline for any IT organization that wants to survive and thrive in a world in which real-time business intelligence is a competitive necessity. Three reasons are driving this:

Data isn't a static thing

According to Gartner, big data can be described by the "Three Vs":[10] volume, velocity, and variety. It's also changing constantly. On Monday, machine learning might be a priority; on Tuesday, you need to focus on predictive analytics. And on Friday, you're processing transactions. Your infrastructure needs to be able to support all these different workloads, equally well. With DataOps, you can quickly create new models, reprioritize workloads, and extract value from your data by promoting communication and collaboration.

Technology is not enough

Data science and the technology that supports it is getting stronger every day. But these tools are only good if they are applied in a consistent and reliable way.

---

10 *http://www.gartner.com/it-glossary/big-data/*

Greater agility is needed

The agility needed today is much more than what was needed in the 1990s, which is when the data-warehousing architecture and best practices emerged. Organizational agility around data is much, much faster today—so many times faster, in fact, that we need to change the very cadence of the data organization itself.

DataOps is actually a very natural way to approach data access and infrastructure when building a data environment or data lake from scratch. Because of that, newer companies embrace DataOps much more quickly and easily than established companies, which need to dramatically shift their existing practices and way of thinking about data. Many of these newer companies were born when DevOps became the norm and so they intrinsically possess an aversion to a silo-fication culture. As a result, adopting DataOps for their data needs has been a natural course of evolution; their DNA demands it. Facebook was again a great example of this. In 2007, product releases at Facebook happened every week. As a result, there was an expectation that the data from these launches would be immediately available. Taking weeks and months to have access to this data was not acceptable. In such an environment, and with such demand for agility, a DataOps culture became an absolute necessity, not just a nice-to-have feature.

In more traditional companies, corporate policies around security and control, in particular, must change. Established companies worry: how do I ensure that sensitive data remains safe and private if it's available to everyone? DataOps requires many businesses to comply with strict data governance regulations. These are all legitimate concerns.

However, these concerns can be solved with software and technology, which is what we've tried to do at Qubole. We discuss this more in Chapter 5.

In This Book

In this book, we explain what is required to become a truly data-driven organization that adopts a self-service data culture. You'll read about the organizational, cultural, and—of course—technical transformations needed to get there, along with actionable advice. Finally, we've profiled five famously leading companies on their data-driven journeys: Facebook, Twitter, Uber, eBay, and LinkedIn.

CHAPTER 2

Data and Data Infrastructure

A Brief History of Data

The nature of data has changed dramatically over the past three decades. In the 1990s, data that most enterprises used for business intelligence was *transactional*, generated by business processes and business applications. Examples of these applications included Enterprise Resource Planning (ERP) applications and Customer Relationship Management (CRM) systems, among others. This type of structured data included the data stored in data warehouses, Online Transaction Processing (OLTP) systems, Oracle and Teradata databases, and other types of conventional data repositories.

The need to manage transaction data dictated the way we built data infrastructures until the advent of the internet, when we started to see *interaction data*, or data generated by interactions between people or between machines. This semi-structured or unstructured data included web pages as well as the various types of social media, which were generated and consumed by people rather than machines. Music, video, pictures, social media comments, and so on fall into this category.

And then sensors began to play the interaction game, leading to machines interacting with other machines or other people. This type of interaction data was primarily created by machines monitoring various aspects of the environments: servers, networks, thermostats, lights, fitness devices, and so forth.

If we think back again to Gartner's Three Vs of big data—volume, velocity, and variety—we realize that the interaction data has a much higher velocity, volume, and variety than the traditional transactional data created by business applications. That data is also of very high value to businesses. Figure 2-1 offers a simple illustration of the evolution of data from transactional to interaction.

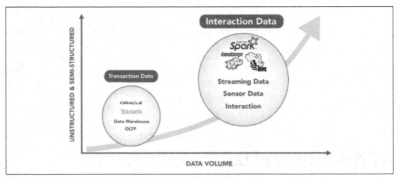

Figure 2-1. The changing nature of data (source: Qubole)

In this chapter, we explore the drivers of big data and how organizations can get the most out of all the different kinds of data they now routinely collect. We'll also present a maturity model that shows the steps that organizations should take to achieve data-driven status.

The Evolution of Data to "Big Data"

International Data Corporation estimates that global data doubles in size every two years, and that by 2020, it will amount to more than 44 trillion gigabytes. That's a tenfold increase from 2013.[1]

The *velocity* at which new data is created is also increasing. Half a billion tweets are sent every day (*http://www.internetlivestats.com/twitter-statistics/*), and 300 hours of video are uploaded every minute to YouTube (*http://www.statisticbrain.com/youtube-statistics/*). These are truly mind-boggling numbers.

At the same time, this data is not always structured, so it has a lot of *variety* to it, ranging from semi-structured application logs, machine-generated logs, and sensor data to more unstructured con-

---

[1] *http://www.emc.com/leadership/digital-universe/2014iview/executive-summary.htm*

tent such as pictures, videos, social media comments, and other user-generated content.

At the very core, the rise of interaction data is driven by the convergence of two technological trends of the past two decades: connectivity and proliferation of data-producing devices. Let's take a look at each:

We live on a planet that is increasingly connected
Within the past decade, the communications infrastructure that connects us has progressed by leaps and bounds. The pipes and the technologies that carry information from one point to another are becoming better, bigger, and faster. Figure 2-2 shows the progress of connectivity on mobile technologies.[2]

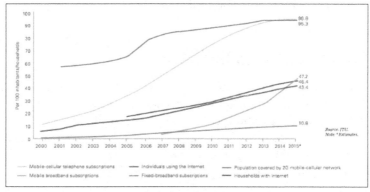

Figure 2-2. Increasing mobile bandwidth around the world (source: Qubole)

We have witnessed the innovation and proliferation of data-producing devices that take advantage of this connectivity
Today's powerful and global communications infrastructure helps us communicate, create, and consume data as never before. We now have at our fingertips devices of various sorts and forms, ranging from communication and information devices such as smart phones to monitoring devices such as personal health instruments, smart electric meters, and so on. These devices are always on, have powerful abilities to collect loads of data, and are always connected.

---

2 *https://www.itu.int/en/ITU-D/Statistics/Documents/facts/ICTFactsFigures2015.pdf*

The combination of these two trends—the connectivity infrastructure and the proliferation of data-producing devices—has created the infrastructure to enable applications to create and gather data like never before. It is this confluence that has given rise to big data (Figure 2-3).

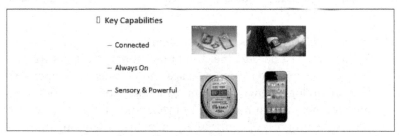

Figure 2-3. Devices are now always on, connected, and powerful (source: Qubole)

Challenges with Big Data

The biggest challenge in big data initiatives? Connecting employees to the *right data* and helping them understand *what to do with that data* to make better business decisions. According to KPMG, more than half of executives (54 percent) say the top barrier to success is identifying what data to collect. And 85 percent say they don't know how to analyze the data they have collected.[3]

Gartner predicts that 60 percent of big data projects over the next year will fail to go beyond the pilot stage and will be abandoned.[4] Why is that? We at Qubole have analyzed why big data projects fail and have come up with some hypotheses (see Figure 2-4).

Big data is difficult for many reasons. Many industries that have not traditionally used data are still trying to figure out how to use it. At the other end of the spectrum, there are industries that have embraced data but still struggle with how...well, *big*, it is. A lot of this struggle has to do with the new systems and technologies that have emerged to address the need for big data. This innovation does not seem to be slowing down. As a result, it is very difficult for busi-

---

3 *https://infocus.emc.com/william_schmarzo/kpmg-survey-firms-struggle-with-big-data/*
4 *http://www.gartner.com/newsroom/id/3130017*

nesses to have the vision and expertise to build and operate these platforms.

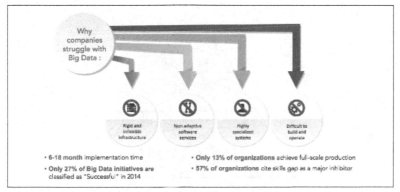

Figure 2-4. Hypotheses for failure of big data initiatives (source: Qubole)

Added to this is the large investments in infrastructure that need to be made to put together these platforms. Between the lack of expertise, large investments in infrastructure, and a constantly shifting technology landscape, many businesses become caught up in the confusion and begin to see projects flounder and fail.

Despite these challenges, CEOs named data and analytics as a top-three investment priority for the next three years.[5]

The Evolution of Analytics

With more and more data being available, the need for advanced analytics has also increased tremendously. What began with descriptive analytics in the transaction-processing world has evolved to prescriptive analytics in today's data-rich environments (see Figure 2-5). Previously, in descriptive analyses, we would look at business intelligence (BI) dashboards to describe what has happened. It was like looking in a car's rearview mirror. But with new practices such as machine learning, companies can now perform predictive analyses: what will happen. And even prescriptive analyses: what actions can you take based on that prediction?

---

5 *https://assets.kpmg.com/content/dam/kpmg/pdf/2016/07/2016-ceo-survey.pdf*

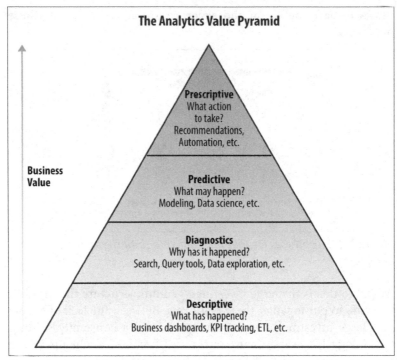

Figure 2-5. Analytics value escalator

Here is how Gartner describes the four types of analytics:[6]

Descriptive
> This was provided by analyzing transactional databases, and gives hindsight: the ability to look back on events and see what happened. For example, your business might have had unexpectedly poor quarterly results, and you want the details of exactly what happened.

Diagnostic
> Taking a step further, transactional data could be analyzed to answer the question: why did it happen? We're moving from hindsight into insight. So *why* did your sales drop precipitously? You can analyze the data to find out the reason.

---

6 *http://www.gartner.com/it-glossary/predictive-analytics/*

Predictive

Now we're interested in mining our data to see what *will* happen. You identified the problem in the previous stage: you had a supply-chain problem that resulted in diminished inventory—so you didn't have enough product to satisfy customer demand. You can use the data to predict if it will happen again this month.

Prescriptive

Finally, we want to use data to discover how we can *make* something happen. How do you stimulate sales for the next quarter given what the data tells you about customer demands in different geographies compared to your distribution-chain capabilities in those areas?

Components of a Big Data Infrastructure

The simultaneous changing nature of data and analytics has caused different technologies to emerge. One such technology umbrella is Hadoop, which has delivered remarkably well on scalability, cost effectiveness, and variety of analysis frameworks. The Hadoop ecosystem is built on the vision of creating a highly scalable modern data platform atop commodity computing servers. It is also built via a vibrant open source community. With its emergence, for the first time, companies can cost-effectively collect as much data as they want. The question has changed from *what data can be stored?* to *why can't we collect that data as well?* This is truly a disruption.

A complete and integrated platform includes the components that make up the data "supply chain" as well as a range of different kinds of analyses.

The Data "Supply Chain"

The following list presents the four components that represent the supply chain of data:

Ingest

The process of importing, transferring, loading, and processing data for later use or storage in a database is called *data ingestion*. It involves loading raw data into the repository. A variety of tools on the market can help you automate the ingestion of data.

Data preparation and cleansing

A successful big data analysis requires more than just raw data. It requires good, high-quality data. There's an old axiom: garbage in, garbage out. So, this aspect of a big data infrastructure involves taking the raw data that has been ingested, altering and modifying files as needed, and formatting them to fit into the data repository. Historically, the cleansing and preparation of data has been a long, arduous, time-consuming process. However, new tools and technologies now exist to help with this process.

Analysis

This involves modeling data with the goal of discovering useful information, suggesting conclusions, and supporting decision-making.

Egress

Many of the outputs of the analyses are consumed by humans, machines, or other systems. So, there are tools that provide access and connectors to other systems, making it possible to upload these artifacts.

Different Types of Analyses (and Related Tools)

A number of different types of analyses have emerged as organizations attempt to make sense of big data. Additionally, an ecosystem of tools has grown up to support these different types of analyses. Let's take a look:

Ad hoc analyses

These are business analyses, typically deployed by analysts, that are designed to answer a single, specific business question. The product of ad hoc analysis is usually a statistical model, analytic report, or other type of data summary. Typically, analysts who perform ad hoc analyses take the answers they get and iterate, exploring the data to find actionable intelligence and meaning. Within the Hadoop ecosystem, SQL engines such as Presto and Impala have emerged to address the needs of ad hoc analyses.

Machine learning

This type of analysis is typically performed by data scientists. By applying machine learning algorithms, they discover patterns implicit in the data. Whereas SQL engines form the foundations of ad hoc analysis, machine learning applies statistical techniques to build and train models on datasets with the intention of applying those models on new data points in order to generate predictions and insights about new data. Apache Spark has emerged as a leading technology when it comes to machine learning.

Deep learning
Also known as deep-structured learning, hierarchical learning, or deep-machine learning) is a branch of machine learning based on a set of algorithms that attempt to model high-level abstractions in data. Google's TensorFlow has gained a lot of traction when it comes to deep learning in big data analyses. Examples of deriving structure out of unstructured data abound in this area; for example, image recognition, natural-language processing of tweets or comments, and so on.

Pipelines for data cleansing and driving dashboards
A data pipeline is infrastructure—plumbing, really—for reliably capturing raw data from websites, mobile apps, and devices; massaging and enriching it with other data sets; and then converting it into a payload of data and metadata that can be used to drive other analysis or populate Key Performance Indicator (KPI) dashboards for operational needs. Hive and Hadoop have become very popular over the years for creating data pipelines.

Putting together an infrastructure capable of supporting all of this is a complex endeavor. Happily, the emergence of cloud and cloud-based services that offer big data infrastructure on demand takes out this complexity and allows business to actively seize advantage from analyzing data rather than becoming bogged down building and maintaining an adequate infrastructure. We discuss this in greater detail in Chapter 5.

How Companies Adopt Data: The Maturity Model

How do companies move from traditional models to becoming data-driven enterprises? Qubole has created a five-step maturity model that outlines the phases that a company typically goes through when it first encounters big data. Figure 2-6 depicts this model, followed by a description of each step.

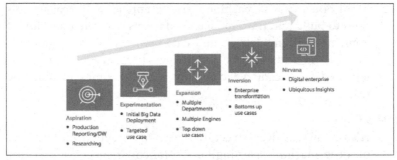

Figure 2-6. The Qubole Data-Driven Maturity Model (source: Qubole)

Stage 1: Aspiration

At this stage, a company is typically using a traditional data warehouse with production reporting and ad hoc analyses.

The signs that you are a Stage 1 company include: having a large number of apps that are collecting growing volumes of data; researching big data, but not investing in it yet; hiring big data engineers; actively contracting with Software-as-a-Service (SaaS) applications and go-to-market products; and gathering budget requirements for big data initiatives.

You also face certain challenges if you're in Stage 1. You don't know what you don't know. You are typically afraid of the unknown. You're legitimately worried about the competitive landscape. Added to that, you are unsure of what the total cost of ownership (TCO) of a big data initiative will be. You know you need to come up with a plan to reap positive return on investment (ROI). And you might also at this time be suffering from internal organizational or cultural conflicts.

The classic sign of a Stage 1 company is that the data team acts as a conduit to the data, and all employees must to go through that team to access data.

The key to getting from Stage 1 to Stage 2 is to not think too big. Rather than worrying about how to change to a DataOps culture, begin by focusing on one problem you have that might be solved by a big data initiative.

Stage 2: Experiment

In this stage, you deploy your first big data initiative. This is typically small and targeted at one specific problem that you hope to solve.

You know you're in Stage 2 if you have successfully identified a big data initiative. The project should have a name, a business objective, and an executive sponsor. You probably haven't yet decided on a platform, and you don't have a clear strategy for going forward. That comes in Stage 3. Numerous challenges still need to be circumvented in this stage.

Here are some typical characteristics of Stage 2 companies:

- They don't know the potential pitfalls ahead. Because of that, they are confused about how to proceed.
- They lack the resources and skills to manage the big data project. This is extremely common in a labor market in which people with big data skills are snapped up at exorbitant rates.
- They cannot expand beyond the initial success. This is usually because the initial project was not designed to scale, and expanding it proves too complex.
- They don't have a clearly defined support plan.
- They lack cross-group collaboration.
- They have not defined the budget.
- They're unclear about the security requirements.

Stage 3: Expansion

In this stage, multiple projects are using big data, so you have the foundation for a big data infrastructure. You have created a roadmap for building out teams to support the environment.

You also face a plethora of possible projects. These typically are "top-down" projects—that is, they come from high up in the organization, from executives or directors. You are focused on scalability and automation, but you're not yet evaluating new technologies to see if they can help you. However, you do have the capacity and resources to meet future needs, and have won management buy-in for the project on your existing infrastructure.

As far as challenges go, here's what Stage 3 companies often encounter:

- A skills gap: needing access to more specialized talent
- Difficulty prioritizing possible projects
- No budget or roadmap to keep TCO within reasonable limits
- Difficulty keeping up with the speed of innovation

Getting from Stage 3 to Stage 4 is the hardest transition to make. At Stage 3, people throughout the organization are clamoring for data, and you realize that having a centralized team being the conduit to the data and infrastructure puts a tremendous amount of pressure on that team by making it a bottleneck for the company's big data initiatives. You need to find a way to invert your current model, and open up infrastructure resources to everyone. The concept of Data-Ops (as defined in Chapter 1) is suddenly very relevant, and you begin talking about possibly deploying a data lake.

All the pain involved in Stage 3 pushes you to invest in new technologies, and to shift your corporate mindset and culture. You absolutely begin thinking of self-service infrastructure at this time and looking at the data team as a data platform team. You're ready to move to Stage 4.

Stage 4: Inversion

It is at this stage that you achieve an enterprise transformation and begin seeing "bottoms-up" use cases—meaning employees are identifying projects for big data themselves rather than depending on executives to commission them. All of this is good. But there is still pain.

You know you are in Stage 4 if you have spent many months building a cluster and have invested a considerable amount of money, but you no longer feel in control. Your users used to be happy with the big data infrastructure but now they complain. You're also simultaneously seeing high growth in your business—which means more customers and more data—and you're finding it difficult if not impossible to scale quickly. This results in massive queuing for data. You're not able to serve your "customers"—employees, and lines of business are not getting the insight they need to make decisions.

Stage 4 companies worry about the following:

- Not meeting Service-Level Agreements (SLAs)
- Not being able to grow the database
- Not being able to control rising costs

Stage 5: Nirvana

If you've reached this stage, you're on par with the Facebooks and Googles of the world. You are a truly data-driven enterprise with ubiquitous insights. Your business has been successfully transformed.

How Facebook Moved Through the Stages of Data Maturity

The data team evolved from a service team to a platform team, building self-service tools in the process.

In 2011, Facebook had tens of petabytes (PB) stored. For the time, that was a lot. But compare that to 2015, when 600 TB are ingested every day, 10 PB are processed every day, and 300 PB in total is stored.

During the six years from 2011 to 2017, Facebook has experienced a huge growth in data scale, the number of users, and the ambitions of what it wants to do with its data platform.

Today, if Facebook hasn't reached the "nirvana" of the Qubole Data-Driven Maturity Model, it is quite close. The journey has been an interesting one.

The journey begins in August 2007. The company was still in Stage 1, the "aspirational" state of its self-service journey. The data team was a service organization running use cases for anyone in the company that needed answers from the data. Most of the use cases revolved around Extract, Transform, and Load (ETL). Product and business teams would come to the centralized data team, and the data team's members would figure out how to get the data to the team that requested it. Simultaneously, the data team would need to understand what kind of infrastructure and processing support it needed to get to that data.

In effect, the data team was a conduit, or gateway, to the data needed by the product and business teams. The technical architecture was a data warehouse into which results were dumped—mostly summaries. The data was collected from the web services running the Facebook application and the application logs collected were dumped onto file storage for further processing. Facebook was using a homegrown infrastructure to process that data, and then summarize it into smaller datasets that were then loaded into the data warehouse.

The problem was that the data team had become a bottleneck. Anytime requestors in the organization needed a new dataset, they had to come back to the data team and describe what they needed. The data team would write more code using its homegrown tools, process logs, create the data, and pass it back to the requestors.

Another problem was that fine-grained data was disregarded and thrown away. The data team summarized data at a very coarse level of granularity, very much limited to ETL and use cases. Executives wanted decision-making to be data driven but given this state of affairs, it was very difficult to incorporate data into the decision-making process. Facebook knew it needed to change this, and put together an infrastructure that would scale with the company.

Facebook achieved Stage 2 at the time it was launching its Ad platform. This was not a coincidence. With the advertising network, Facebook had an urgent need for collecting clickstream data, and using it to understand what ads should be shown at what time to which people. Facebook knew it had to think a little differently, so it began to experiment with Hadoop.

This was between August 2007 and January 2008, and what Facebook did at that point had profound implications. The Hadoop data lake made it possible to retain raw-level data and put it online. Hive was developed at this time to make that data lake widely accessible. In effect, the data team evolved during this stage from a service team to a platform team, building self-service tools in the process. Facebook realized it could now open up this architecture to the engineering team and make the data accessible, obviating the need of the data team to be a conduit to this data.

Moving to this stage was successful on two levels. First, developer productivity shot up, and the barriers to people collecting the right levels of data and performing analyses were reduced dramatically.

On the data side, it meant that it became extremely easy to use APIs to log data without a lot of approvals and internal processes.

For Facebook, it was interesting to see how some seemingly simple decisions had a magnifying effect. Self-service turned out to be something that paid back the organization in spades. But, it now had to worry about putting controls and safeguards in place that would reward good users and train the bad ones on how to use the system properly.

At this point, Facebook moved into Stage 3. Using metadata services along with Hive, users could look at both the data and the metadata. This happened in late 2008, and it really opened up the power of big data to a lot more use cases within Facebook. Now analysts could perform ad hoc analyses—something they couldn't do before—but because the tools were still very technical, product managers and other business users who were interested in data still had some trouble getting to it. In Stage 3, Facebook began to think hard about how to build a truly self-service platform for everyone in the company.

Facebook reached Stage 4 in 2009. It developed UI interfaces that were friendly and intuitive enough for nontechnical users to master. As usage ramped up, so did the challenges that come with self-service: demand for faster processing, a demand for swifter loading response times, and other user demands. There was also the proliferation of data, and, as the infrastructure was used by more employees, deciding how to share the infrastructure equitably, and preventing users from running bad queries became very important.

Although one could argue that "Nirvana" (Stage 5) is always just out of reach, one could argue that Facebook today is close. It has addressed many of the challenges that arose in earlier stages and continues to push the limits of what's possible with big data.

Summary

The drivers of big data—the fact that we live in an increasingly connected world, and the number and types of different data-producing devices are multiplying—will only grow more intense as time goes by. By moving to a self-service culture, organizations can get the most out of all the different kinds of data they now routinely collect. But to do this successfully, organizations need to advance step by step through the Qubole self-service maturity model presented in this chapter.

CHAPTER 3

Data Warehouses Versus Data Lakes: A Primer

Chapters 1 and 2 introduced the idea of a data-driven organization and defined the concept of DataOps within the context of big data initiatives. Now, it's time to take a step back and explore some other basic but important concepts. One of our most important tasks at this point is to clearly delineate the differences between *data warehouses* and *data lakes*.

When I give talks about self-service data, questions inevitably come up. What distinguishes a data lake from a data warehouse? Do I need to choose between them or do I need both? What are current best practices for setting up the relationship between a data warehouse and a data lake? This chapter answers these questions and more, and delves into a detailed explanation of why augmenting your existing data warehouse with a data lake is the best path to take given the current state of maturity of the various technologies.

Data Warehouse: A Definition

At its most basic, a data warehouse is a central repository for all the data that is collected in an organization's business systems. Data is extracted, transformed, and loaded (known as ETL) into a data warehouse, which supports applications for reporting, analytics, and data mining on this extracted and curated dataset (Figure 3-1). The previous generation of data infrastructure centered on data warehouses and was based on technologies such as Teradata, Oracle, Neteeza, Greenplum, and Vertica, among others.

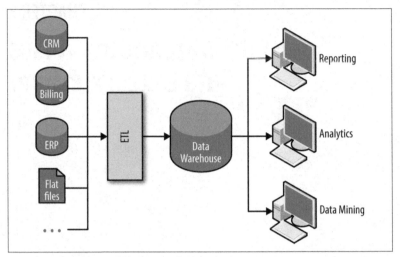

Figure 3-1. A typical data warehouse

In the past, enterprises would take raw data as well as processed data; perform ETL on it using engines such as Ab Inito, Informatica, and others; and then load it into the data warehouse to be consumed by business analysts or users. However, with the increase in data volumes, this approach creates two problems: first, the analysts have no access to the original raw data and are limited to using the extracted subset from the data warehouse; and second, only processing on structured data is possible in a data warehouse. No deep learning applications or analytics using unstructured information is feasible. Both of these problems create severe limitations in making data and processing broadly accessible.

In a data warehouse–centric world, if the defined structure of the data in the warehouse did not fit into your analysis or you wanted to analyze unstructured content, you were simply out of luck. You would need to reach out to the data team to put in your data request, wait until it had the raw datasets, processed them, and derived the information and the structure in which you were interested. Then, you waited for the data team to load it into the data warehouse. This was a very slow process.

This traditional process made you fundamentally less agile. After all, business analysts and users had to depend on data professionals to process the raw data and get it into the warehouse in its desired (structured) form. In many cases, the original raw data would simply be thrown away or archived due to lack of available storage; it could not be used for analysis or verification after ETL was performed.

For all these reasons and more, possessing only a data warehouse in a modern data architecture to support a data-driven enterprise is simply not optimal.

What Is a Data Lake?

The term data lake was first coined by James Dixon, founder and chief technology officer of Pentaho, back in 2010. Dixon posited that a data lake is a storage repository that holds a vast amount of raw data in its native format until it is needed.

Data lakes address the shortcomings of data warehouses in two ways. First, in data lakes, the data can be stored in structured, semi-structured, or unstructured formats. Second, the data schema is decided upon reading, rather than loading, or writing, the data. You can thus always change the schema if there is extra information or structures that you need from the raw data, leading to greater organizational agility. This also means that the data is quickly available because it does not have to be curated before it can be consumed by the processing engines.

Because of the cost effectiveness of data lakes, there is never any need to throw away or archive the raw data. *It is always there* should any of your users want to revisit it.

All of these points—cost effective storage of all content, different types of processing abilities on both structured and unstructured data, fast availability of data, agility, and flexibility—are essential as organizations move toward a self-service data infrastructure (see Figure 3-2).

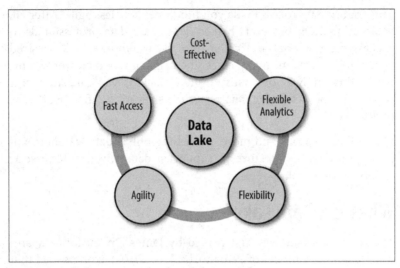

Figure 3-2. Advantages of a data lake

Key Differences Between Data Lakes and Data Warehouses

More and more businesses are augmenting their data warehouses with data lakes to make their big data truly self-service.

There are eight basic differences between data lakes and data warehouses. Here are the most important among them:

- The type of data that goes into them
- How much processing the data undergoes during ingestion
- How many different types of processing can be done on this data

Figure 3-3 shows the main differences between a data lake and a data warehouse.

Data warehouses continue to be popular because they are very mature technologies, having been around since the 1990s. Additionally, they work well with the tools business analysts and users have become accustomed to when using dashboards or other kinds of mechanisms through which they can consume insights from the resident data. In fact, for certain use cases, data warehouses perform very well because the data is completely curated and structured to answer certain query patterns quickly.

Data Warehouse	vs.	Data Lake
structured, processed	**Data**	structured / semi-structured / unstructured, raw
schema-on-write	**Processing**	schema-on-read
expensive for large data volumes	**Storage**	designed for low-cost storage
less agile, fixed configuration	**Agility**	highly agile, configure and reconfigure as needed
mature	**Security**	maturing
business professionals	**Users**	data scientists et al.
SQL	**Types of Queries**	Multiple types: programmatic access, machine learning, SQL, graph analysis, deep learning, etc.
mature	**Tool Integration**	maturing

Figure 3-3. Differences between data lakes and data warehouses

As a result, data warehouses continue to hold sway at most organizations. But more and more businesses are running into the roadblocks we mentioned earlier. To overcome them, they are augmenting their data warehouses with data lakes to make their big data truly self-service. In many cases, the lake can serve as a staging area for the data warehouse, which then acts as the more curated data to be analyzed.

When Facebook's Data Warehouse Ran Out of Steam

When I first arrived at Facebook in 2007, we had only a data warehouse, which was curated and maintained by the central data team. But this turned out to limit the amount of actionable insight Facebook could get from all the data it was collecting.

Although the data team would perform ETL and load data into the data warehouse, the amount of data was growing so fast that the team had to throw the raw data away after the curated version was loaded.

By creating a Hadoop-based data lake, Facebook was able to load all of its data into the still-centralized repository, and with the schema-upon-read nature of the architecture, Facebook was able to add different processing engines to our data lake, support different types of analysis, make more data available faster and create an agile and flexible self-service model for all of its employees without having to delete or archive any of its raw data.

Is Using Either/Or a Possible Strategy?

Another question that invariably comes up after I have defined the difference between data lakes and data warehouses is this: Do you really need both, or can you use one or the other to solve your data self-service initiatives? The answer to this question is no—not at this time. Considering the stage of maturity of the technologies involved, you need both.

It is true that data warehouses are slowly accumulating many of the features that formerly were found only in data lakes. But the economies of scale are such that even if you were able to do everything you needed with your big data in a data warehouse, it would be so prohibitively expensive that you would soon wish you had created a separate data lake in addition to your data warehouse. In addition, with an architecture that assumes and uses a schema definition for optimized storage, it is a more difficult transformation for traditional data warehousing technologies to morph into data lakes. They also architecturally are based on proprietary storage formats that are strongly coupled with their processing engines, and creating a more decoupled architecture that the data lakes can support is very difficult to achieve.

On the other hand, as Hadoop architectures morph and mature in the open source world, they are also borrowing concepts that have been made popular in data warehouses, such as columnar formats and special processing engines for speed. Indeed, over time, the architectures have begun to merge so that one architecture can encompass the high-performance, low-cost, and highly integrated capabilities required to support big data analytics today. And the emergence of engines like Presto and Impala specifically address the issues of performance in data lakes that open source technologies like Hadoop and Hive have traditionally faced.

Common Misconceptions

When I talk about data lakes and data warehouses, I find some common misconceptions exist, even among technically sophisticated designers, architects, and engineers. Here are a few of them.

Data Warehouses are Dead

One of the most common misconceptions about the data warehouse–data lake relationship is that after you have a data lake, a data warehouse is no longer needed. That is, as soon as you reach your end goal of a data lake, you can close down your data warehouse. This is not currently true, although the world is moving in this direction. The data lake simply does not support everything that a data warehouse does. The primary concern is the maturing of the integration with the ecosystem tools. Data warehouses, being the previous generation technology, are more mature as far as their integration with business intelligence (BI), ETL, and other SQL-based data tools is concerned. Data lakes are still maturing in this respect.

Data Warehouses Will Become Data Lakes

Others believe that as data warehouses begin to add features of data lakes, that a full data lake will not be needed. This is also a fallacy, and given the architectural coupling that is inherent in the data warehousing technologies (mentioned later in this section), it is an unlikely outcome. Organizations that go down that path will ultimately realize they could have done things a lot more cost effectively and that they'd be a much more agile business if they'd built a data lake. Perhaps most important, they would be very limited in the types of analytics they could do with a data warehouses.

As Chapter 2 informs us, there are four different types of analytics: descriptive, diagnostic, predictive, and prescriptive, as illustrated in Figure 3-4.

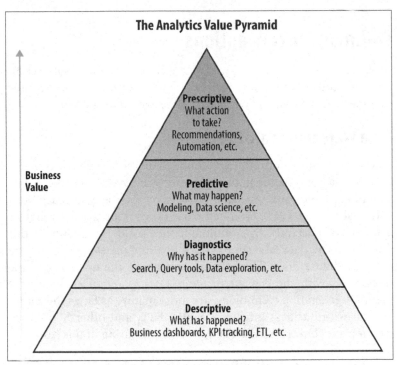

Figure 3-4. Analytics value pyramid

Although SQL queries can cover some of these types of analytics— most notably in the descriptive and diagnostic area, they can't cover all of them. This is a serious limitation for companies that want to get the most out of their big data initiatives.

A key reason why different processing engines and different types of analyses are possible in a data lake architecture is because data formats are decoupled from the considerations of the processing engines. In the data lake, data is stored in an open format such as comma-separated values (CSV) or JavaScript Object Notation (JSON, an open-standard format that uses human-readable text to transmit data objects consisting of attribute–value pairs) or compressed sparse format (CSC) formats, not closed formats that are coupled to the processing engine. This means that on the same raw data, you can apply different data processing engines.

Conversely, with data warehouses, after data has been structured and stored in the format proprietary to that technology, it is not possible to use engines other than the proprietary SQL engine to process it.

Take, for example, data that has been placed into a Vertica data warehouse. After it is in the Vertica columnar format, data can be understood only by Vertica's processing engine. You cannot take data that is stored in that environment and apply deep learning or machine learning toolkits on it. You must extract it from Vertica and feed it into any of these libraries, which is an inherently time-consuming process that needs help from the data team.

In data lakes, because data processing engines are disconnected from the data, you have choices as to which engines to use to analyze the data. You can use Spark for machine learning, or Google's TensorFlow on the same open format dataset, or natural-language processing (NLP) libraries in the open data formats.

Difficulty Finding Qualified Personnel

One of the biggest challenges an organization faces when building a data lake is finding qualified personnel. Your existing data team will be very familiar with data warehouses, which have been around for a long time, are fairly mature, and have strong integration with the ecosystem of data tools.

But the data lake architecture is less mature. Technology is still evolving in that space, and expertise consequently is more difficult to find. Typically, data lake projects are initiated by the data engineering team. This creates challenges for going to a self-service infrastructure for all use cases using a data lake.

So, it takes more people and expertise to create a data lake, precisely because of the immaturity, and the limited time data lakes have been in the public consciousness—just over six years to date. In addition, the operational tools to manage data lakes are also evolving, although they have made significant strides in the past few years. A lot of progress has been gained on managing access controls, monitoring costs, assigning chargebacks to different teams based on their usage, and managing storage usage, as well as other aspects of managing data lakes. But still it is much more difficult for companies to support data lakes from an operational perspective.

Summary

In summary, data lakes offer a lot more flexibility and agility to organizations—characteristics that are very important to building a data-driven enterprise. They are able to do it a fraction of the cost as compared to attempting to do it with a data warehouse. In many ways data warehouses are turning into the data marts of yesteryear. On the other hand, data lake architectures are less mature and can have significant operational complexity. However, the cloud plays a big role in reducing that complexity, so that every enterprise can aspire to include a data lake architecture in the data infrastructure strategy. With the cloud and cloud-based Software-as-a-Service platforms for data lakes, organizations can eliminate the complexity of operations and at the same time enjoy tremendous total-cost-of-ownership benefits while building a data lake architecture.

We cover this in more detail in Chapter 6.

CHAPTER 4

Building a Data-Driven Organization

The previous chapters define what a data-driven organization is, and they discuss the importance of building one to remain competitive. Now, we'll spend some time talking about the practical steps needed to build a data-driven organization.

In our opinion, a data-driven organization should possess three things:

- A culture in which everyone buys into the idea of using data to make business decisions
- An organizational structure that supports a data-driven culture
- Technology that supports a data-driven culture and makes data self-service

We cover the first two points in this chapter and discuss the roles and responsibilities of the employees who form the vital cogs in the engine that drives the data-driven organization—from data producers, to data scientists, to engineers, to analysts, to business users.

The next chapter devotes itself to the technology needed to support a data-driven culture.

Creating a Self-Service Culture

The most important—and arguably the most difficult—aspect of transitioning to a data-driven organization that practices DataOps is the cultural shift required to move to a data mindset. This shift entails identifying and building a cultural framework that enables all the people involved in a data initiative—from the producers of the data, to the people who build the models, to the people who analyze it, to the employees who use it in their jobs—to collaborate on making data the heart of organizational decision-making. Though the technology that makes this collaboration and data access easy is very important, it is just one of the considerations. A key focus area in this transition are the employees and the organization. After you achieve a true self-service, data-driven culture, as discussed in Chapter 1, you should experience a significant competitive boost to your business.

Fostering a Culture of Data-Driven Decision-Making

To succeed at becoming a data-driven organization, your employees should always use data to start, continue, or conclude every single business decision, no matter how major or minor.

What drives companies to have a successful data-driven culture? It's important to understand that it's not necessarily about the data itself. That's secondary. The technology itself comes in third. Data-driven decision-making is first and foremost about the organization.

Regardless of whether you have acknowledged it, your business already has a culture of decision-making. That culture might not be geared toward a data-driven approach. All too many companies subscribe to the "HIPPO" (highest-paid person in the office) method of decision-making, whereby the senior person in the meeting gets to make the final choice. Needless to say, this HIPPO can be wrong. But unless you have the data as well as the permission coming from the very top of the organization to argue back, that decision stands.

And herein lies the key: to succeed at becoming a data-driven organization, your employees should *always* use data to start, continue, or conclude every single business decision, no matter how major or minor. This kind of inquisitive culture should drive everyone on the data team—including IT, data engineers, data scientists, and data analysts—to continually enhance and refine the tools that business users need to inform their decisions. Because data is accessed and used a lot in this type of environment, the organization should encourage and deploy people, processes, and technologies that minimize barriers to this access.

You know that you have successfully shifted to a data-driven culture when data-driven initiatives begin coming from the bottom of the organization rather than the top. It is common in the beginning to find a top-level sponsor in an organization to bless a data project or a change that incorporates the use of data in certain functions. For example, a common function in enterprises that is rapidly shifting to being data driven is marketing. A CMO of a company can set that tone by making it mandatory that new creatives and campaigns be experimented with and tested to gather data on their effectiveness as opposed to just relying on gut-feeling and intuition. That message gives primacy to data, and that sentiment then flows to the rest of the marketing organization. The initial data project also helps as a proving ground of the importance of data to the executives and helps them to see the immediate benefits of using data. In addition, a successful initial data project becomes a role model for how you can use data in other projects.

Although such top-down measures or projects are necessary to initiate the change, eventually, a company truly becomes data driven when there is a bottom-up demand for self-service data access. For that to happen, it is necessary that the tools and mechanisms are there to support this bottom-up interest among employees. For example, after the self-service tools and processes are in place, employees in the marketing department might actually use the data collected from previous campaigns to come up with a hypothesis of what a new campaign or message should look like. In essence, data begins to become part of the muscle memory of the entire department.

A key driver to enable a data culture is to make it easy for the data team to capture all of the data in the organization. An enterprise has a plethora of data sources, both internal and external. These can range from different business applications, product applications, public and private customer interaction points, monitoring systems, third-party data providers, and many others. These systems are set up for operational reasons, with collecting data for analytics being an afterthought. As a result, the natural tendency is to not capture any of this data, far less consolidating it in one place. The valuable data from all of these sources, therefore, continues to remain in its silo. In the process, the organization loses many opportunities of deriving insights or optimizations by putting data from different sources together.

The first step toward overcoming this challenge is to take an inventory of all your data sources and create a common data-capture infrastructure that is standard across the company and that lays out the correct way to capture and log the data. Everyone should use those standards. The next step is to consolidate all of the data so that all consumers of data in the organization know where to go to find it. This is what we did at Facebook, and, indeed, all of Facebook's massive data stores are still in a centralized location.

Creating a consolidated data repository helps everyone to collaborate around data. You will have data analysts who analyze the data and feed the results back into the business. They ask questions like, "How do I use data to improve my products?" and further, "How do I get data back from my customers to change the features of the product, perhaps personalize them?" With standardization of capture and consolidation of data, it becomes very easy for data engineers to write self-service applications that support that feedback loop. The business users then use those analyses to make strategic decisions.

The executive team also will benefit from standardized and centralized data. Top people in the company typically don't have enough time, or the skills, to analyze data themselves. Yet they need data to inform their decisions, perhaps more than anyone else in the company. So, it makes sense to build business dashboards so that the executive team can access the data in a timely and self-service manner. For example, for any given company, there will be business metrics that reflect important trends and statistics in the business: sales, prices, customer churn, and so on. Keeping these statistics up-to-the-minute and accessible to senior executives can benefit your business enormously.

It's important to understand that different stakeholders will buy into using data for different reasons. You must first identify who all the stakeholders are. Then, you must understand what will motivate them to begin using data to make decisions.

Tips on Building a Data-Driven Culture

Following are five tips on how to build a data-driven culture.

1. Hire data visionaries

You need people who see the "big picture" and understand all the ways that employees can use data to improve the business. Although this certainly includes analyzing marketing, sales, and customer data, it doesn't end there. Data-driven decisions can help with internal operations, such as making customer service and support more efficient, and cutting costs from inventory, for example. And it all begins by hiring people who are open minded about what the data will tell them regarding the way forward—people who have a vision.

2. Organize your data into a single data store accessible to everyone

All of the data in the universe won't help if that data is inaccessible to the people who need it to make business decisions. A data-driven company consolidates its data while keeping it continuously up to date so that employees have access to the most accurate information at any given point in time. This means eliminating data silos and effectively democratizing data access. There are, of course, always data security and compliance issues, which we discuss in Chapter 6 But making data available to everyone is an important feature of a self-service data culture. Always allow employees to see the data that affects their work. They need to see this not only at a granular level, but also in a holistic way that helps them to understand the bigger picture. Doing this will make your employees more informed, skilled, and enthusiastic about using data to improve the business.

3. Empower all employees

All employees should feel comfortable taking initiative when it comes to suggesting ways that data can be used. This kind of mentality goes well beyond just using data, of course. If you build a company where *all* employees feel free to give opinions—as long as they are backed up by data—even if those opinions contradict senior executives' assumptions, you are building an organization where the best ideas will naturally gravitate to the top and keep you competitive in even the fastest-moving markets.

4. Invest in the right self-service data tools

Your data, even if readily accessible, won't help your business much if most of your employees can't understand it or don't apply it to business problems. You can solve this problem by investing in the right data tools, which we discuss in more detail in Chapter 5. You should pick tools based on your goals, but as a starting point, your tools should make it easy for your employees to access, share, and analyze data. You might want tools that can be directly embedded into the business tools you already use; for example, Excel and Tableau. And make sure to invest in training for these tools. Having an "intuitive interface" isn't enough. Do your employees understand basic principles of data analysis, transformation, statistics, and visualization? To achieve return on investment on your tools, your employees must understand exactly what capabilities each tool offers. Training can be live, video-based, or online, and should use a shared data store so that employees can compare their data discoveries and explorations with one another.

5. Hold employees accountable

Technology will take you only so far. You also need to put incentives in place to encourage employees to use the technology and tools. You also should have a way to measure and grade progress toward a self-service data culture. This means holding employees accountable for their actions and progress when they effectively use data to drive business decisions. Only when you reward employees for actions based on data will you achieve true cultural transformation.

The collaborative, *social* dimension of a self-service, data-driven culture is also not to be underestimated. Without it, you will fail, and your investments in software, data processing tools, and platforms will be wasted. Yet, although many organizations pay lip service to this notion of collaboration and openness, few follow through with the appropriate actions. Keep in mind that data doesn't belong to IT, data scientists, or analysts. It belongs to everyone in the business. So, your tools need to allow all employees to create their own analyses and visualizations and share their discoveries with their colleagues.

Potential Roadblocks to Becoming a Self-Service Data Culture

The most common roadblock to becoming a self-service data culture is that you'll face resistance from the team of people who have traditionally been the conduit between the data and the users. They might say, "We can't let everyone access the data. There are security issues and compliance issues." Although these are valid issues to raise, you can solve them by means of technology. Today, technologies that tie user identity to access control policies as well as technologies that capture audit logs can easily address such objections. Don't let these issues become crutches that prevent you from transforming into a true self-service culture.

Another potential challenge—we saw this at Facebook—is that as you open up your data stores to everyone, you might find that you don't have the infrastructure to support such broad-based access. There are either limits of scale or it becomes extremely expensive to process all the queries coming in. You need to address this issue by using infrastructure that can scale in a cost-effective manner. (More on this in Chapter 5.)

But, keep in mind that most of the roadblocks will be put up by the traditional centralized data team being hesitant to give up control over other users. Because this is the most problematic challenge, companies need to focus on this team, perhaps reorganizing or retooling it. Remove any bottlenecks and make it possible for this centralized team to become the heroes in the self-service culture as opposed to the obstructionists. So, it's really a psychological as well as an organizational challenge.

Creating a data-driven culture is not always easy, but the benefits it provides are real and significant. Big data is transforming the ways that organizations conduct business, so it should come as little surprise that it has a role to play in changing your culture, as well.

Organizational Structure That Supports a Self-Service Culture

Organizationally, how do you support a data-driven company? In most successful data-driven organizations there is a central data team that publishes data and manages the infrastructure used to publish that data. In others, there might be multiple data teams embedded in different departments, each catering to the needs of that department. Ironically, the latter model is typically less successful in creating a data-driven culture, even though data teams are there in each department. The reason is simple: such an organization creates low connectivity between the different departments and ends up creating data silos. A strong, functional, central data team is therefore extremely important in creating connectivity between the different departments of an organization. They usually publish the most important datasets, making sure that there is a single source of truth that underpins the analyses.

Consuming these datasets are the analysts that are typically embedded in the different departments of the organization, helping those departments to ask questions from the datasets. Think of this as a hub-and-spoke structure, as depicted in Figure 4-1. The embedded data analysts have the domain knowledge about the business function and also understand the datasets that can help them answer those questions. They have the ability to convert the language of systems to the language of the business.

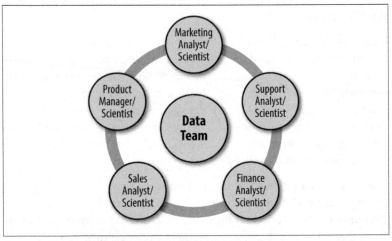

Figure 4-1. Organizational hub-and-spoke model (source: Qubole)

This skill is critical because the two languages are very different. The business wants to ask questions such as the following:

- Which geographic regions of my business are the best to invest in?
- What is the size of the market?

- Who is the competition?
- What are the best opportunities today?

You then need analysts who can take those business questions and convert them into a series of questions to ask the data. Thus, data analysts would translate these questions into SQL or other commands to pull the relevant data from the data stores.

At Facebook, we had a centralized data team. Then, we had analysts embedded in every product team. We also took care that all the analysts had a central forum at which they could meet and communicate what they were doing, allowing data intelligence to flow through the entire organization. Essentially, this model transmitted the data-driven DNA of the self-service organizational culture throughout the company.

How the Hub-and-Spoke Model Works

The people embedded in the business units can be either data analysts or data scientists, depending on how sophisticated the business unit's requirements are. If deep learning or machine learning is required at the business-unit level, you need data scientists in that role; if business users requires reporting and answers to business questions, data analysts are more appropriate to embed.

Domain knowledge of individual business functions is essential for the data analysts and data scientists embedded in the functional teams. Analysts need to be outstanding at understanding a domain and converting it to technical questions to be asked of the data. They become the bridge between the data and the line-of-business users. Data analysts, as a result, get a lot of exposure to the functional area on one side, and to the metadata about the datasets on the other. They understand how those are interlinked, a crucial skill to be able to use the data effectively to answer business questions.

For example, at Facebook, we had data analysts embedded in the product teams: within Growth, Ads, and so on. Those data analysts quickly got up to speed on the specific issues facing the teams in which they were embedded.

The coupling between the analysts themselves and the central data team is quite important. There is a natural dependency of the analysts on the data team because the latter is the primary publisher of curated datasets. However, equally important is the interaction between the analysts in the different functions. Such interactions help them in pushing for collaboration and data sharing as opposed to creating data silos. A typical way of achieving this interaction is by creating a forum within the central data team that allows all data professionals, from data scientists to data engineers to data analysts, to discuss their data usage and what they are trying to do.

Finally, these professionals are supported by the central data team. The latter are eventually responsible for maintaining the infrastructure and providing the access to datasets needed by the data users. If any link in this "value chain" of data is weak, friction arises in the path to attainment of a true data-driven culture. Chief data officers are usually the folks with the ultimate responsibility of nurturing and growing this value chain of data.

Training Is Essential for Data Analysts

Because they need to have equally deep knowledge of the data, the data tools, and the domain of the function in which they are embedded, data analysts require extensive training. The training can be formal classroom training and also involve shadowing of more experienced analysts. A key aspect of the job is learning the Key Performance Indicators (KPIs) for the particular domain. How does the marketing department, for example, measure success? Or the key goals of the operations teams and how they measure success? Understanding the goals, strategies, and tactics used to achieve those goals and finally the measurement of those achievements are essential for the data analysts to understand in order to be effective in translating the business questions into data queries.

Roles and Responsibilities

Now that you understand what a self-service culture is and how to organize your data professionals into a hub-and-spoke model, it's time to examine more closely how the specific roles and responsibilities of data professionals are organized.

Naturally, you want the best people on the job. And every business, of course, has different needs and goals, meaning each data team that is assembled will be composed of different types of people with different capabilities. However, some things are common to all data teams no matter what business they support. Carefully specifying the roles and responsibilities of each member of the team will avoid conflict and inefficiency.

In this section, we outline the best way to assemble a data team that can meet the challenges you face in the big data world.

Figure 4-2 shows the major *personas* that are a part of the data team in a data-centric business.

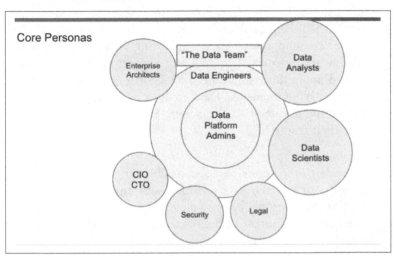

Figure 4-2. Core personas of the data team (source: Qubole)

What's a persona?

The persona is a profile of a job role. It is *not* a person or a job title. In fact, one employee might represent multiple personas (in a small company). Alternatively, one persona might be split across multiple people in a larger enterprise. Understanding personas is important because it allows you to comprehend their pain points, what they care about, and their ultimate responsibilities.

If you understand personas, you can pinpoint which messages are likely to be the most relevant to the person you are talking to as you try to effect a transformation into a data-driven enterprise. It's very important to understand that this is *not* a hierarchy, but a collaborative team that works together in the hub-and-spoke model described in the previous section. Here are the personas you're likely to come across:

Data analysts

These data professionals are typically embedded in line-of-business or functional groups. Their job is to transform business questions into queries on the available data sets. They are data users, but not programmers (as opposed to data scientists —read on). These are the people who are most familiar with how the business is run, what the strategic objectives are, and how data fits in. They have a deep understanding of the practices that will help achieve executives' goals and can effectively utilize frontend tools. They might not fully understand the inner workings of a data analytics algorithm, but they know how to apply those functions and algorithms to the questions they are trying to answer. Data analysts are able to use the data and communicate with the senior management the findings from their research.

Data engineers

These data professionals are responsible for getting data into the platform so that the data scientists and analysts can get to it. They are responsible for providing mechanisms to capture data from different sources in the organization including end products. In addition, they are typically responsible for publishing core datasets in the organizations after cleaning and transforming any captured data. In short, data engineers make sure that the data is available, curated, and cleansed. They're generally a part of IT, reporting to the CIO or VP of engineering. Because the data engineers are so intrinsically linked to data ingestion and processing, it's vital that they keep open lines of communication with data scientists and analysts in order to fully enable analytics further downstream. They might also be dependent on application developers in order to put instrumentation in the products for capturing data.

Data scientists

These are the members of the data team involved in statistics, machine learning, and deep learning. They rely on advanced data mining tools and are the ones responsible for putting together predictive and prescriptive analytics. Tools such as R, Python, and Scala are their favorite environments, and they possess deep understanding of deep learning and machine learning toolkits. In some industries, they might even be referred to as quants because they tend to have a strong mathematics background.

Chief data officer
> The person who oversees operations of the entire data team and who typically reports directly to the CEO or the CTO.

Compliance and security teams
> These professionals ensure that compliance mandates like HIPAA are met through periodic audits.

Data platform administrators
> These data professionals manage the data infrastructure. They are responsible for production DBMSs, data warehouses, and big data infrastructure. Administrators manage the infrastructure so that it is functioning well, has enough capacity, gives adequate quality of service to the different teams using the infrastructure, and so on. They also are the people who control access rights to data. They establish the implementation of access control policies and security policies of an organization. They are also ultimately tasked with providing the infrastructure and tools in the most economical manner.

Line-of-business users
> The ultimate users of the data to make decisions. They are provided with reports, ad hoc analysis tools, and so on. These are the people that take analysis and act on it; for example, in the case of marketing, campaign managers might look at the ROIs of certain campaigns and decide to move their budgets accordingly.

Of course, companies that sell data as products are different. When a business's products—what it makes or sells—are primarily made up of data, the personas will be much more product-centric. IT is less important, and product managers are much more important in such environments. Everyone in the organization is much more technical, so data knowledge is typically distributed through the lines of business.

A Central Forum for Coming Together

Despite the distributed nature of the data users in the organization, it's important to understand that there is no hierarchy. Instead, the organization provides a mechanism for coming together and sharing, collaborating, and learning from one another. All these roles have their place in strategic data initiatives. For example, Facebook announced a growth initiative, and the data scientists developed the models through which data analysts, and, ultimately, business users could complete analyses that would help the company grow, whether by campaigns to acquire new users, new product development, or other means.

This central forum enabled the Facebook data users to speak a common language and provided common definitions of data, such as what constituted an address or phone number. The team also could engage in cross-functional analyses, in which an analysis developed for and embedded in the Ads team could use data analysis results created by the Groups team.

The hub-and-spoke structure facilitates these conversations and disperses the knowledge throughout the organization. This is much more effective than a traditional command-and-control model.

Summary

In this chapter, we discussed ways to transform your business into a data-driven organization with a self-service culture. We discussed the different organization roles and responsibilities, and presented the very important hub-and-spoke organizational structure needed to support such a transformation. By learning and implementing these concepts, your business will be on its way to becoming truly data driven.

CHAPTER 5

Putting Together the Infrastructure to Make Data Self-Service

Now that you understand how to assemble your data-driven organization and what the respective roles and responsibilities are in the hub-and-spoke model, the next step is to understand the technology infrastructure necessary to make data self-service.

Technology That Supports the Self-Service Model

It used to be that big data initiatives involving large datasets, Hadoop, and open source technologies were mysterious and complex processes best left to PhDs. But this has changed. In the last few years, the cloud coupled with powerful yet easy-to-use querying and reporting tools has made self-service possible. This includes enabling self-service data for data analysts as well as business users who lack a technical background.

Gartner (*http://www.gartner.com/it-glossary/self-service-analytics/*) defines self-service analytics as follows:

> [a] form of business intelligence (BI) in which line-of-business professionals are enabled and encouraged to perform queries and generate reports on their own, with nominal IT support.

Putting the appropriate infrastructure in place is an essential part of achieving self-service. The mindset has to be thus: as a data-driven organization, we will publish *all* data without thinking of how it will be used. Then, the infrastructure platforms and analysis tools all need to be self-service and data universally available.

Tools Used by Producers and Consumers of Data

Chapter 4 looked at all of the different personas within the data-driven organization. Here we will limit our discussion to tools used by the four personas who are the "producers" and "consumers" of data. As you would expect, the different personas use different types of tools and interfaces to interact with data. The differences arise because of the varying types of analyses and the level of technical depth needed to do those analyses. The different data consumers in a data-driven enterprise are as follows:

Business users

Business users have a very strong understanding of the business processes and the Key Performance Indicators (KPIs) that they need to monitor and operate the business. They are able to best consume the data in the form of dashboards created by visualization tools and business intelligence (BI) tools such as Tableau. Excel, of course, remains a very important tool in these users' toolkits, as well. Beyond that, these consumers do not have a sophisticated knowledge of SQL. Nor do they understand deep statistical or machine learning algorithms; for example, a campaign manager in the marketing function of an enterprise would consume the data from KPI dashboards built around metrics from campaigns such as reach, conversion rates, and return on investment (ROI). Sometimes, these metrics might also be embedded within the tools that they use to manage business functions. For example, in marketing, some of these dashboards might be provided by the marketing automation software. At other times, especially when the analysis depends on correlating data from different sources, BI and dashboarding tools play a big part in making the data consumable as insights to the business users.

Data analysts

Data analysts are people who can take the business questions posed by the business users and understand the datasets needed to answer those questions. They also know how to frame those questions using data tools such as SQL. They heavily use metadata tools to discover data. Typically, the data and metadata is provided by the data engineers to them. They are able to do interactive, ad hoc analyses on these data sets using SQL. Finally, they are able to put the results of their analyses into dashboards using BI and visualization tools—artifacts that are consumed by the business users. These users play a crucial role in understanding the business processes of the organization and the KPIs and know how to build those from data.

Data scientists

Data scientists, or "quants," as they are often called, are people who come from deep math, statistics, and machine learning backgrounds. Not only are they well versed in SQL, metadata, and discovery tools, but they are also knowledgeable about machine learning and statistical libraries available through tools such as Python and R. These users are experiencing a continuous evolution of tools and interfaces that can create an integrated user experience that subsumes the diversity of languages and frameworks that they use. New-age visualization and dashboarding tools, popularly known as "notebooks," are very popular in this user group. Zeppelin and Jupyter are examples of such tools. This group also adopts Python and Scala as languages to do deeper analyses. Many of these users are found in advanced research teams in the enterprise.

Data engineers

Data engineers are the professionals who assemble, create, and publish datasets for all the aforementioned consumers. They are constantly making sure that the data is well curated and reliable. They are also responsible for ingesting the data from different sources and ensuring that the metadata uses a set of common nomenclatures in describing datasets and fields so that the data consumers can easily discover the datasets in which they are interested. This persona best works with software development kits (SDKs) and uses tools and libraries to cleanse datasets. Sometimes, they do this by using Extract, Transform, and Load (ETL) tools such as Informatica, Talend, and other new-age data-wrangling tools, and at other times through home-grown systems written in Python or other languages.

Developers

Last but not least, in organizations that are creating products based on data, developers are big consumers. They typically use programming languages and parallel processing frameworks to create analytical applications. These applications could be based on deep learning and artificial intelligence frameworks. (Popular ones include Google's TensorFlow.) Or, they could be based on simple number-crunching or correlation analyses such as are done in recommendation applications. The interfaces to data for this group are SDKs in different languages such as Java, Python, PHP, and so on.

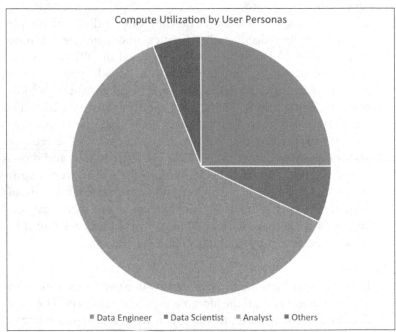

Figure 5-1. Compute resource utilization by user persona (source: Qubole, 2016)

The Importance of a Complete and Integrated Data Infrastructure

Supporting the various analyses and interfaces that are used by different types of data consumers in the enterprise means that the data infrastructure needs to be well integrated with all these tools. In addition, the infrastructure needs to support different types of engines that are optimized for certain workloads. For example, the needs of ad hoc SQL workloads are very different from the needs of deep statistical machine learning workloads. As a result, in the open source big data world, engines such as Presto and Impala are becoming more and more used for interactive ad hoc queries, whereas engines like Spark are being used for machine learning and data science workloads.

A modern data infrastructure, therefore, needs to be built on a data lake architecture, in which the data is published in an open format. Different analytical engines (Hadoop, Spark, Hive, Presto, and Impala) are then able to process the data for the different data consumers' requirements. Here's a sampling of some of the popular engines:

Hadoop

Apache Hadoop is an open source software framework used for distributed storage and processing of big datasets using the MapReduce programming model. Hadoop is a great tool for developers programming in Java. There are also some interfaces such as Cascading available to reduce the complexity of programming on top of Hadoop. In addition to MapReduce, Hadoop also supports processing frameworks such as Tez that might be more suitable for workloads that are more interactive.

Spark

Apache Spark is a fast and general engine for big data processing, with built-in modules for streaming, SQL, machine learning, and graph processing. Spark, which started out as an in-memory engine, has had very strong ties to data structures used in machine learning and data frames, and supports integration with machine learning libraries that are available in environments like Python or Scala. As a result, it has become a tool of choice for many data scientists and consumers of notebooks.

Hive

Apache Hive is a data warehouse (*https://en.wikipedia.org/wiki/
Data_warehouse*) infrastructure built on top of Hadoop (*https://
en.wikipedia.org/wiki/Hadoop*) for providing data summariza-
tion, query, and analysis. Hive gives an SQL-like interface
(*https://en.wikipedia.org/wiki/SQL*) to query data stored in various databases and file systems that integrate with Hadoop. Hive
supports complex SQL and is used heavily in ETL workloads by
data engineers because it is very fault resistant. This is essential
because if a job goes wrong, engineers don't want to have to run
the entire workload again. Hive has become especially strong in
creating data pipelines for ETL workloads. It also is used for ad
hoc analysis on large datasets through the SQL interface. Along
with Tez, Hive is becoming more and more suitable for ad hoc
analysis workloads, as well.

Presto

An open source distributed SQL query engine for running
interactive analytic queries, you can use Presto to run queries
against data sources of all sizes. Presto addresses the needs of
low-latency queries, and is very commonly used for ad hoc
analyses by data analysts who want a quick answer so that they
can continue on and ask other, related questions. Based on a
similar architecture as Google's BigQuery, Presto has a streaming architecture where data is streamed, and thus doesn't support complex SQL, although simple SQL is supported. Simple
SQL with limited number of joined datasets is quite common in
interactive analysis authored by data analysts.

Impala

An open source, massively parallel processing (MPP) SQL
query engine, Impala was developed by Cloudera to analyze
data stored in clusters running Hadoop. Built along a similar
architecture to Presto, analysts also use Impala to run quick
queries against data with the intent of iterating until they reach
their goal, whatever that might be.

These engines have different compute utilizations (see Figure 5-2)
and average cluster lifetime (Figure 5-3).

A modern data infrastructure also must support rich SDKs, integration with other tools, and common metadata across the different

processing engines in order to make data self-service for a data-driven enterprise.

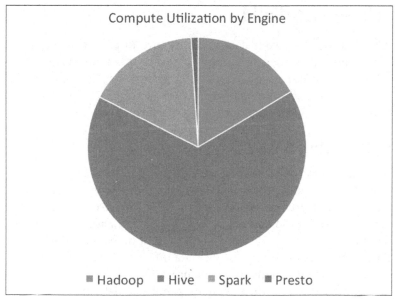

Figure 5-2. Compute resource utilization by engine (source: Qubole, 2016)

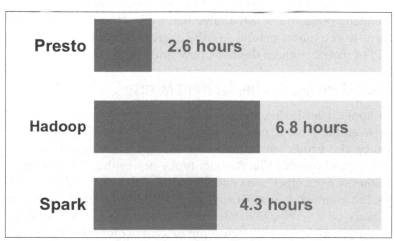

Figure 5-3. Average cluster lifetime by engine (source: Qubole, 2016)

The Importance of Resource Sharing in a Self-Service World

After you open up your data infrastructure to an entire enterprise and empower its users, a fair way to share this multitenant infrastructure becomes essential. You need the infrastructure to perform well for everyone without forcing users to wait in long queues or have their queries held up due to poor performance.

Multitenancy and Fair Sharing

In a self-service world, the infrastructure is multitenant. That is, different departments, groups, and users share the same infrastructure. As a result, it becomes important that the infrastructure is shared fairly between the different users and their use cases. A notion of fair sharing might mean equal use or might be based on priorities. Either way, it is important for the data infrastructure team to define this contract between them and the users. One of the mechanisms to create this contract is through quotas: not just data quotas but also quotas on the amount of compute resources. In addition, there needs to be a feedback mechanism to the consumers on how much infrastructure they are using and the associated costs. After all, the company needs to know the value that it is getting from its investment in the infrastructure. Are the queries paying off in whatever KPI or metric has been deemed important?

Protecting Against Inadvertent Misuse

Although fair sharing and quota mechanisms define the contract between the providers of the infrastructure and the users, multitenancy also brings with it scenarios in which uses might inadvertently grossly violate that contract to the degree that they take away resources from other users and impact the infrastructure's availability. For example, an inexperienced user could forget to add a filter in a query on a very large dataset and in the process consume all the resources, leaving not enough compute capacity for other workloads —some of which might also be time sensitive. For any multitenant infrastructure to succeed, solving this problem is imperative. In other words, the infrastructure must be "hardened."

This can involve simple steps like being vigilant for certain patterns of queries; making sure each transformation has a filter; putting limits on the amount of data that can be queried; and so forth. In addition, the infrastructure itself should be able to predict such patterns and shut them down before they cause damage to the other users. Apart from hardening, another common approach is to create and maintain separate infrastructures for very time-sensitive, strict SLA, "production" workloads and for the ad hoc workloads, so that you achieve at least some level of isolation from failures.

Security and Governance

Making data self-service means also that security and governance around data needs to be reimagined.

In the traditional approach, you had the data team sitting between the infrastructure and the users. This data team acted as the gateway to the data, and thus security and governance was not difficult. It was a manual process: humans deciding what data to share with whom. Business users would make requests for data—say, the marketing department wanted three years of quarter-to-quarter comparison of sales to North American customers—and the data team would decide based on security considerations and compliance requirements what data could actually be released.

But when the intermediaries are taken out of the model—when the data is made self-service—security (controlling access) and governance (performing audits) become critical.

All enterprises have infrastructure to support user identity. Typically, enterprises depend on Active Directory, Lightweight Directory Access Protocol (LDAP) servers, or single sign-on products that store user identities and are used for authenticating users. When making data self-service, you need to tie those identities to the access policies around data. For example, your policies could say employees in certain roles could look only at certain tables and datasets, or certain columns and fields within those tables.

To make this manageable, it is important to ensure that all of the data access happens through a single gateway. When this is done, all of the access control mappings, from the user identities to the data-access policies as well as all the collection of audit logs, can be easily achieved. With such an architecture in place, self-service does not become chaotic and the guarantees around security and governance become easier to enforce.

A number of different tools can help achieve this architecture. For example, in the Apache Hadoop ecosystem, Apache Ranger is one such tool. Irrespective of the tool used, what is important is that the access is through a controlled set of gateways or access points where all the intelligence and monitoring for security and governance can be built.

Self Help Support for Users

Providing feedback to data users on the effectiveness of their queries is essential in making data self-service. After all, you have several different types of users. Some will be experts in the use of data analysis tools; others will not. When you create a self-service infrastructure, you are essentially getting different types of users executing their queries on the infrastructure. By giving them feedback on the effectiveness of their data requests, you gradually raise the bar of sophistication in your data-driven organization. It also leads to a model in which users do not always have to go to the experts to understand their failures or to tune their analyses better.

Giving feedback on errors is particularly essential. If you don't tell users when they make errors, they will keep returning to data experts and asking what went wrong. This wastes everyone's time. Make sure to include a feedback loop for errors in your organization's self-service model.

Authoring and Tuning of Queries

The platform has to make the authoring of workloads—and the tuning of them to run efficiently—easy for the users. In terms of authoring, the platform can monitor queries and transformations from different users and utilize that information to build recommendations that help guide other users while authoring their workloads. These could be recommendations on datasets and fields that are correlated together, or recommendations on datasets that might have already summarized the desired analysis.

In addition to authoring help, tuning the authored workloads also becomes crucial. The platform therefore needs to support tools that can give users a clear picture of where the bottleneck in a particular workload is. In the Apache Hadoop ecosystem, tools such as Dr. Elephant from LinkedIn help solve this need. A self-service data platform must provide these tools as part of the platform so that the users can author and tune their workloads themselves.

Monitoring Resources and Chargebacks

When you create a self-service infrastructure, unless there are quotas, or ways to give feedback to the various teams about their usage of resources, employees will inevitably run too many queries. And unless you make the cost of what they are doing apparent, the infrastructure will begin experiencing bottlenecks. As a result, it becomes necessary to monitor the resource utilization of the infrastructure by various teams and projects. You already have user identities, which you use when applying policies for security and governance. You need some further structure in place when monitoring usage for quotas and chargebacks. For example, which teams do certain business users and analysts report to? What organizations are those teams part of? What is the structure of the line-of-business operations?

When you know all that, you can allocate resources to any organizational unit you like. You can even allocate down to the individual or project level if you want by monitoring and charging usage of the data infrastructure back to a specific user or project within a specific team within a specific business unit.

For example, suppose that you want to analyze the success of a particular marketing campaign. So, you query the data related to that campaign. Because your usage of resources is being monitored, you would be told that the project is using 10 percent of the business's compute resources, and that exceeds the established limit. These limits, or quotas, can be hard or soft. For example, a soft quota could be five percent of a business's compute resources; if usage of the cluster goes beyond that number, you get an alert. But if your usage goes up to six percent or seven percent, your usage will be shut down, and your jobs queued behind those of other department's or lines of business's projects.

These quotas are necessarily tied to chargebacks. The team is notified how much their activities are costing the organization (or in many cases, the individual department or even the team). These notifications give teams a quantitative basis for judging the ROI of their projects. The visibility and feedback helps them prioritize what is important and what is not. Most organizations build their own tools for this kind of monitoring.

The "Big Compute Crunch": How Facebook Allocates Data Infrastructure Resources

Facebook once made the decision to open up its rich trove of data stores to everyone in the organization—an essential step in becoming the data-driven business it is. But this caused a problem. The analytics infrastructure team called this the "Big Compute Crunch." Basically, the infrastructure became strained from overuse. So popular was the idea that anyone could query data that the team quickly became overwhelmed.

Facebook decided to deal with the problem in three ways:

Made query processing more efficient
In effect, Facebook had to do more with less. So, the team created Presto. Presto, which eventually became open sourced, is a distributed SQL query engine for running interactive analytic queries against data sources of all sizes. Although Hive was a great improvement over attempting to write queries in MapReduce, Presto took things a step further by making interactive queries much faster and more efficient.

Put checks into place about infrastructure usage
The second thing that they did was to put a series of checks and balances in place to ensure that users were more deliberate about the analyses they were running. Facebook created a sophisticated self-service platform that provides insight into who is using what and why, and provides feedback so that users understand they are using shared infrastructure—one that is finite and fairly expensive, not infinite and free.

To do this, Facebook created what it called "namespaces," or logical groupings of pipelines, tables, and analyses, along with a set of tools. It dedicated administration of each namespace to someone within each product team who had the most visibility into the organization's priorities and workloads. That administrator made decisions about what queries were important and which were less important. Facebook set up Service-Level Agreements (SLAs) and sequenced the high-priority jobs in a queue based on the policy decisions of the namespace admins. This was important so that users could understand the impact and make the correct choices about the use of resources. Everyone could see the queue, see the analyses that their colleagues had done, and share and optimize the resources.

Using the Cloud to Make Data Self Service

The good news is that you don't need to go through all the complexity and growing pains that Facebook went through to achieve a self-service data infrastructure and culture. A cloud platform can provide many of the required attributes for a big data platform right out of the gate. Instead of reinventing the wheel that Facebook already did, you can easily get to a self-service place much faster.

Cloud's elasticity, scalability, and other attributes allow you to achieve multitenancy, fair-sharing, centralized security and governance, self-service user experience and monitoring, and chargebacks much faster and more cost effectively. We discuss this in detail in Chapter 6.

Summary

Like all new technologies and tools, the self-service model has some barriers to adoption. Chief among them: how to allocate resources to all the different employees who wish to use the business's constrained—usually by cost—data resources. Going forward, companies seeking to implement a self-service model need to find ways to monitor and charge for use of data resources. The fact that this is infinitely easier in the cloud points to where the future of the data-driven organization is going.

CHAPTER 6

Cloud Architecture and Data Infrastructure-as-a-Service

Creating a self-service data culture within your organization can seem daunting. You need to recognize the technical and structural requirements of providing data access to all as well as the need for resource monitoring and chargebacks to individual groups. And you must accomplish this while maintaining robust security and compliance controls. However, all these requirements become much easier to achieve in the cloud. This chapter looks at the efficiency and agility your organization can achieve by moving your data-driven initiatives to the cloud.

Five Properties of the Cloud

There are five properties of the cloud that make it a uniquely suitable infrastructure for building a self-service data platform:

- Scalability
- Elasticity
- Self-service and collaboration
- Cost efficiencies
- Monitoring and usage-tracking capabilities

In this chapter, we discuss how these properties can help data teams create self-service data platforms.

Scalability

One of the biggest advantages of cloud computing is your ability to quickly expand infrastructure to meet the needs of your organization. Today, because of the cloud, huge amounts of infrastructure are now instantaneously available to any organization. Compute resources can be provisioned in minutes or even less. This is called *scalability*. If you suddenly need, say, a thousand more nodes of compute, you can get it today in the cloud due to the its scaling capabilities. Because of the cloud, large-scale infrastructures are now available to any organization, not just the Facebooks and Googles of the world.

Scalability is frequently talked about at the application layer. Can the infrastructure handle a growing volume of workloads? Can it grow sufficiently and fast enough to meet the expanding demands of the business?

There are two types of scalability the cloud supports: you can scale up (scale vertically) or scale out (horizontally). You scale vertically by creating a larger virtual machine (VM) and transferring a workload to it. Or, you could make the existing VM for the workload bigger. Scaling horizontally means you add more VMs, and divide the load between all of them.

Why is the scalability of cloud important to the self-service model? Because big data workloads can be very large, and very "bursty." They are difficult to run using an on-premises infrastructure because the ability to scale is so limited—you can grow only to the capacity of the physical infrastructure you have already put into place. It's difficult to grow it quickly and cost effectively. And by being limited by infrastructure scalability, organizations can find themselves compromising on data. They use smaller datasets, which result in inferior models and, ultimately, less valuable business insight. With the scalability of the cloud, you can have very large datasets against which to test your hypotheses. And to be true to the vision of a truly data-driven culture, all your data should be kept and made available online. The cloud eliminates the limitations that difficult-to-scale on-premises infrastructures place on you.

Elasticity

Although they are frequently used interchangeably, scalability and elasticity are not synonyms. Both refer to an environment's capability to be flexible—that is, to be able to expand and contract as needed. As workloads increase, this means adding and allocating resources, and "turning off" or reallocating resources as workloads decrease.

Elasticity in cloud infrastructure means that you can harness your hypervisor to provision or de-provision VMs that possess sufficient resources (compute, storage, network, and so on) to meet real-time demand. Scalability, on the other hand, is typically viewed at the workload layer, and focuses on the capability of infrastructure to handle a large volume of workloads as well as its potential to expand to accommodate that growth.

To understand elasticity, you need to appreciate that the cloud has converted infrastructure into APIs. This is a startling innovation. After all, over past decades, traditional datacenter computing had previously trained us to think about infrastructure components as physical entities: machines, networks, storage, and so on. IT was accustomed to a deployment model in which we would first physically "rack up" the infrastructure components, and then load software onto them. When attempting to create self-service data infrastructure under this traditional model, data teams would need to estimate demand for infrastructure, and then provision the compute, storage, networking, and other components needed to support that demand. After that, they had to put this physical infrastructure into racks, test and certify it, and then deploy and test the software. You get the picture. This is the traditional "waterfall" model of IT—a sequential, non-iterative process that pushes development in a steady flow downward (like a waterfall) through the phases of idea, initiation, analysis, design, construction, testing, implementation, and maintenance. This is very out of tune with today's "agile" way of working, which is key to rapid innovation.

As virtualization arrived and grew in popularity in the late 1990s and early 2000s, hardware gradually began to be abstracted into software and we saw the emergence of VMs, virtual storage, even virtual networks. Cloud took these building blocks and essentially married the concepts of virtualization, scalability, and service-oriented architectures (SOAs) to hide all this complexity behind APIs. With the cloud, infrastructure provisioning is no longer a physical activity that takes months to get right. It is now a purely digital activity that takes seconds to complete.

Needless to say, this disruptive change is for the first time challenging the decades-old waterfall model. It enables a much more agile model for data. In this new model, the mindset changes from an "infrastructure-first" mindset to a "workload-first" one. *This is elasticity.* Data users can now focus on what they want to do, and the cloud APIs can give them the desired infrastructure on demand—infrastructure that fits their workloads, that can be scaled up or down based on their workloads, and that can be changed on the fly if the characteristics of their workloads change. All this can be done in a matter of minutes or even seconds.

When working with big data in a self-service culture, this elastic approach to infrastructure is essential for making data available to everyone. That's because of the relative unpredictability in demand for infrastructure when large numbers of users are free to access whatever data they want, whenever they want. Compare this new way of doing things to the times when data was accessible to and controlled by only a few people, and you understand why the cloud is the perfect foundation for self-service.

Cloud elasticity also considerably simplifies and speeds up operations. If you need more compute—more VMs—you spin up more. You can change the capacity and power of these machines on the fly. Nothing is fixed. Agility and flexibility soars. Precisely because you can alter infrastructure on demand, your operations overhead decreases dramatically.

Self-Service and Collaboration

No matter which cloud model you consider—Software as a Service (SaaS), Platform as a Service (PaaS), or Infrastructure as a Service (IaaS)—it has been built around tools that enable self-service and collaboration. Because everything is API-driven, users can choose VMs, storage, and networks as well as other resources without having to request someone else to do it for them. No administrator is needed. And just as elasticity is about flexibility, so is self-service infrastructure: no matter how small or large the workload is, users have the authority to procure the infrastructure they need to run it. And this self-service property makes organizations incredibly agile.

Collaboration naturally follows self-service when we talk about cloud properties. When users are empowered to test their hypotheses or perform ad hoc exploration of data in a data-driven culture, they naturally collaborate. And this is essential when it comes to big data. To successfully operate as a data-driven company, some users are preparing datasets; other users are analyzing those datasets; and still others are taking those analyses and creating long-running data pipelines, dashboards, and Key Performance Indicators (KPIs). Collaboration is essential for any big data initiative to succeed, and the cloud facilitates that.

Cost Effectiveness

Another important property of the cloud is that it's significantly more cost effective than on-premises infrastructure. There are two reasons for that: one, the fees are calculated on a usage model rather than a software-licensing one; and two, your operational costs are much lower because you don't need to maintain an IT operations staff to manage and maintain the infrastructure. In fact, moving to the cloud generally boosts the productivity of IT personnel.

First, the pay-as-you-use model. In the cloud, you pay only for what you use. With on-premises infrastructure, you must purchase and build the infrastructure to accommodate peak workloads. Even if most of the time your usage requirements are generally not high, you must accommodate those peaks or risk running out of resources, which almost always results in a higher total cost of ownership (TCO) than the cloud. For examples, most retailers previously had to build infrastructure to handle the holiday season, which meant that they paid a great deal for infrastructure that was used for two and a half months each year. The rest of the year, that capacity remained dormant. Now, with the cloud, retailers can scale-up in November and December, and then flexibly go back to paying much less for what they need in January and the rest of the year.

Secondly, the TCO of the cloud is reduced because it improves the productivity of IT in general and the DevOps team in particular. You don't need to employ people to manage datacenters, because all of that is done by the cloud provider. In addition, the economies of scale that are achieved by the cloud providers because multiple organizations are using the same infrastructure are passed onto everyone.

One analogy can be found in the way that electricity is produced and consumed. Most businesses don't run their own electrical grids or generators—it would be much more expensive to do that than to simply consume energy from a centralized grid that is used by everyone. It is exactly the same with the cloud.

This cost property is very important to big data. As we've previously mentioned, big data workloads are very bursty—sometimes you need a lot of resources, sometimes you don't need any. To accommodate such workloads with an on-premises infrastructure would by necessity cost more because you'd need to anticipate the peak demand, which would require building the maximum infrastructure beforehand. With the cloud, you can size your infrastructure to what you want to use and reduce your costs substantially. Also, any time you can consume rather than build infrastructure when it comes to big data, the better off you'll be from a cost perspective. With the cloud, you eliminate the need for having huge teams to run the infrastructure, no need for specialists, and the data team becomes that much more productive.

Monitoring and Usage Tracking

To take a full advantage of the cloud and all the aforementioned properties and benefits, organizations need to have full visibility into how their cloud resources are being used. They need to be able to monitor usage of the cloud resources. This brings us to the final cloud property: monitoring and usage tracking. These monitoring capabilities include tools for monitoring machine computing hours, network and storage usage, I/O, and so on.

Remember, the cloud is a multitenant platform. Because of this, the capability to track usage across different tenants and their workloads is essential. There are two important reasons for that. The first is the requirement to ensure fair sharing of the infrastructure, and to protect tenants against misuse of resources by one tenant that affects the Service-Level Agreements (SLAs) of the others. The second reason is that usage monitoring is also used for billing in the cloud model. Because the cloud model moves infrastructure from a capital expense line item in the budget to an operating expense line item, you need to know how much you are using so that you can pay the cloud provider.

The implication of fine-grained usage tracking in the cloud is that IT now has the capability to precisely track and allocate costs and usage of the infrastructure to different business units. This in turn improves the visibility into ROI for using the cloud in various projects or departments and also enables proper governance of resources. You can see, clearly, objectively, and transparently how many resources each line of business or function is getting, for how long, and what the ROI is on their projects.

These abilities are also very important in the context of creating self-service infrastructure for data. If data is made self-service with no monitoring, it soon descends into a state of chaos; a chaos that manifests itself in bad user experiences for the data users and uncontrollable costs for IT. With the cloud's ability to monitor and track usage at a fine level of granularity, these potential problems go away. The self-service data platforms built in the cloud also can use these monitoring properties to build sophisticated charge-back models around data and infrastructure usage in a much more fine-grained and self-service way as compared to on-premises data platforms.

Cloud Architecture

What makes these properties possible is the cloud architecture. Attempting to "lift and shift" from on-premises to the cloud simply doesn't work for big data. Instead, the big data architecture for the cloud is different and needs to be built according to some very specific architectural characteristics.

Separation of Compute and Storage

The data platforms used for processing data that are built for the cloud are different from the data platforms built for on-premises infrastructure. To ensure agility, the cloud must usher in architectural innovation. An important architectural property of the cloud that is important for big data platforms is the separation of compute and storage. Two technologies are the building blocks of this architectural property: virtualization and object stores.

First, virtualization. Virtualization makes compute in the cloud on-demand—VMs can be provisioned and de-provisioned within seconds. Because compute is on-demand and ephemeral, the separation of compute and storage is critical for storage of "persistent" assets such as data. This is achieved by different storage technologies in the cloud that are persistent: block stores and object stores. For large datasets, which are typical when creating data lakes for self-service data, object stores are especially well suited for data storage.

Object storage is an architecture that manages storage as objects instead of as a hierarchy (as filesystems do), or as blocks (as block storage does). In a cloud architecture, you need to store data in object stores and use compute when needed to process data directly from the object stores. The object stores become the place where the data lake is created—basically, all data is dumped into the data lake in its raw format. The cloud-native data platforms then create the compute infrastructure needed to process this data on the fly, whether it be processing for data wrangling, ad hoc analysis, machine learning, or any other analytical application.

Note that this is different from the architectural pattern typically followed by the big data platforms built on-premises. Because of the lack of highly scalable object stores that can support thousands of machines reading data from them and writing data to them, on-premises data-lake architectures stress convergence of compute and storage, as demonstrated in Figure 6-1. The rise of Apache Hadoop —one of the leading big data platforms—was based on the principle that compute and storage should be converged. The same physical machines that store data are the machines that provide the computation for different data applications on that data.

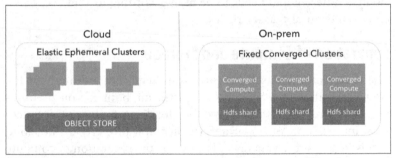

Figure 6-1. Benefits of cloud-based data platforms: elasticity and separation of compute and storage (source: Qubole)

Although this is the standard architecture for on-premises big data platforms, lifting and shifting this architecture to the cloud greatly nullifies the elasticity and flexibility benefits of the cloud. And as we mentioned in the previous sections, those benefits are very important for creating a platform that can make data access self-service.

As a result, cloud object stores and using them to create data lakes is central to the success of creating a self-service data culture. Object stores offer four key benefits:

Scalability

Thousands of VMs can access the object stores for datasets simultaneously. The chief reason for this is the scalable network architecture between the compute tiers and the object store tiers.

Cost effectiveness

The pricing models of storing data in cloud object stores are built around the assumption of long-running usage. On the other hand, the pricing models of compute are built around assumptions of transient usage. As a result, using compute tiers to store data—the way data lakes are created in the converged compute-and-storage world of on-premises data platforms—leads to heavy cost escalations.

Built-in mechanisms for high availability, durability, and disaster recovery

Object stores are built with 99.99 percent availability and 99.999999999 percent data durability design goals. In addition, they are built with support for multiregion data replication. Separation of compute and storage also allows tiers built specifically for storage, such as the object stores, to focus on providing critical SLAs and services that are important for creating reliable and disaster-resistant data lakes at a fraction of the cost of achieving this with converged architectures.

Flexibility

Using object stores to store data and separating compute from storage also means that different type of compute infrastructures can be created for different types of data-processing applications. All of this can be done on demand and can be scaled up and down based on the needs of the computation. To support self-service data access and the unpredictable access patterns that result from that, support for such flexibility becomes critical.

Multitenancy and Security

The cloud was created as a multitenant service. As a result, identity, security, and isolation are concepts that are baked in to the cloud architecture. The requirements for and the abstractions to support authentication and authorization for different cloud resources—compute, object stores, virtual private clouds, and so on—are also different from the needs for on-premises deployments of data platforms.

On-premises big data deployments happen behind the firewall. Because hardware and infrastructure are not virtualized and are not multitenant, there are no strong mechanisms needed to secure infrastructure resources such as machines. Typically, machines are racked-up in the datacenters behind a firewall, and the security is managed by making the firewalls secure. Therefore, for on-premises data platforms, it becomes sufficient to tie user identity stored in identity-management systems such as Active Directory with the authorization policies for accessing data. That is the standard for authentication and authorization to which most data platforms built on-premises adhere.

On the other hand, in the cloud, each API call for provisioning, de-provisioning, or using infrastructure must be authenticated and authorized. It is not sufficient to simply create data-access authorization rules. It is also necessary to tie those rules and the user identity to the right authorization rules for orchestrating infrastructure. As a result, data platforms built for the cloud need to be tightly integrated with the cloud API-level authentication and authorization policies, which are integrations that on-premises data platforms do not need to support.

In addition, the cloud provides mechanisms to encrypt data both in transit and also while the data is stored (at rest). These encryption mechanisms are also tied to external key management systems in which the keys that are used to decrypt the data are stored separately from the cloud infrastructure. Native cloud data platforms are integrated with such mechanisms to provide extra security for highly sensitive datasets that are stored and processed in the cloud.

Why "Lift and Shift" to the Cloud Is Not Possible

For all the aforementioned reasons, a simple "lift and shift" of on-premises data platforms to the cloud does not work and ultimately is not able to take advantage of the cloud elasticity and flexibility. A specific cloud architecture (see Figure 6-2) that takes into account separation of storage and compute as well as multitenancy and security is needed.

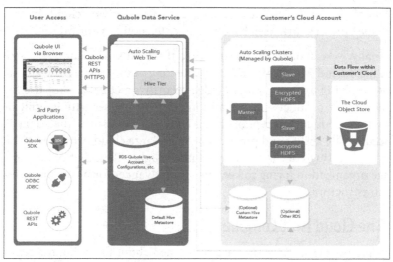

Figure 6-2. Recommended cloud architecture blueprint for a multitenant data platform (source: Qubole)

Objections About the Cloud Refuted

Some organizations have concerns about the cloud that prevent them from transitioning to it, despite all the advantages. There are three primary concerns: security, compliance, and cost. Let's take a closer look at each of these concerns.

"The Cloud Isn't Secure"

Security is the number one concern of organizations thinking of moving to the cloud. They are concerned that their data will be sufficiently secure in it. And, also, given the cloud's multitenant architecture, whether someone else might be able to access it.

Security is always a concern when it comes to data, but in this case, cloud security has improved substantially in recent years, and there is no longer any reason to believe that it is more secure to maintain data on-premises than in the cloud. The reverse, in fact, is true; in the past few years, cloud providers have built strong protections into their services. For example, Amazon has built encryption into Amazon Web Services (AWS), and is easily integrated with key management systems so that the keys and the data are never located in the same location. The multitenancy aspects of the cloud also have been hardened considerably over the years.

You also have the option of creating a virtual private cloud. In this model, the network itself becomes an extension of your firewall.

Finally, you should be assured that the giants of technology like Amazon and Microsoft that are protecting your data in their clouds are applying the same leading-edge security practices as they use for their other products—like Amazon.com. Strong security is built in to the product. Encryption built in to AWS ensures that data is secure, The ability and practices of these large cloud providers to be on the cutting edge of security is much higher than that of an average organization trying to keep up with advances for its on-premises infrastructure.

"The Cloud Isn't Compliant"

When people say this, they are concerned about following the regulations and laws regarding keeping data secure and private. These laws exist at the regional, national, and industry level, and increasingly, there are international regulations, as well. For example, in Europe, you are not allowed to store personal data outside an individual country's border. In the United States, there is the healthcare privacy law, HIPAA, as well as PCI to protect credit card information. In these specific cases and many, many more, you must meet certain standards to avoid data from leaking or being stolen. Compliance used to be a problem for some organizations wanting to move to the cloud, but it isn't any longer.

For example, AWS has been certified in dozens of compliance frameworks, and has put many robust controls in place to ensure data protection. Because organizations build their systems on top of the AWS infrastructure, Amazon shares compliance responsibility with customers. Audit tools are tied to applicable compliance regulations and standards, enabling customers to meet whatever compliance requirements to which they must adhere.

Microsoft's Azure also meets a wide range of international and industry-specific compliance standards, including ISO 27001, HIPAA, FedRAMP, and SOC 1 and SOC 2. Rigorous third-party audits monitor Azure's adherence to the strict requirements mandated by these standards. Azure is also committed to transparency, so you can request audits from certifying third parties at any time.

Ultimately, when it comes to security and compliance, storing data in your own datacenter because you are worried about the cloud's capabilities in these areas is like keeping your money under your mattress at home instead of in the bank. The bank is in the business of protecting assets—much like cloud vendors—and the level of security and best practices are much higher than you could achieve on your own (see Figure 6-3).

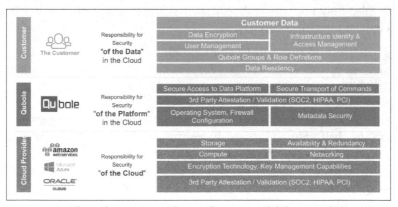

Figure 6-3. Shared security and compliance model for a mult-tenant data platform (source; Qubole)

"The Cloud Is More Expensive"

Some organizations don't accept the argument that the cloud is cheaper. They still take exception to the claims that the cloud results in reduced TCO. Their arguments come down to two specific points. First, because they have sunk costs into their own infrastructures and because those investments have already been made, they should keep using them rather than replicating those capabilities in the cloud. The second argument is that given the cloud pricing is based on a rental model, renting will be more expensive, in the long term, than purchasing. Therefore, they conclude that for most workloads, it makes sense to purchase your own equipment, and to use the cloud merely for bursting events.

The first point is easily challenged. Yes, you've made your investment in your current on-premises datacenter. But this shouldn't preclude you from moving to cloud when the workloads demand it. After all, you can have the best of both worlds by moving your more bursty workloads—which will be your big data workloads—into the cloud, and keeping your more predictable workloads on premises.

The second point is a weak one, too, because cloud vendors are coming up with extremely favorable long-term pricing wherein they give hefty discounts on rental prices in return for a commitment to use their resources for longer periods of subscription. In the end, having a longer-term contract with a cloud provider is going to be much cheaper than investing in your own datacenter because of the efficiencies of scale that a cloud provider has. Added to that, big data is inherently unpredictable and bursty. You would need to move to cloud at some stage anyway.

There's a third point in favor of cloud: as the scale of the cloud— and, more important, competition for customers—increases, prices are dropping rapidly. For example, in the past four years (*https:// www.cloudyn.com/blog/analyzing-aws-ec2-price-drops-over-the- past-5-years/*), Amazon has cut its compute prices on leading instances by half. Storage costs have dropped to one-fifth (*https:// aws.amazon.com/ru/blogs/aws/aws-storage-update-s3-glacier-price- reductions/*) of what they were four years ago. And these prices will only come down further as time goes on and the cloud industry matures.

What About a Private Cloud?

Some organizations might ask at this point, "what about a private cloud?" Granted, the cloud is the right architecture for big data workloads, for all the reasons we've discussed throughout this chapter: scalability, elasticity, cost effectiveness, and so on. But, must it be the public cloud? Why shouldn't we build our own private cloud?

The main reason to go with public over private cloud: economies of scale. True, you'd get the architectural advantages of the cloud. But unless you are a very, very large organization, you will not be able to match the economies of scale of a public cloud provider. Which means that it will cost you more to build a private cloud than to rent a public one. This will only become more true as the public cloud footprint continues to grow, as it inevitably will. Few companies will be able to sustain comparable scale.

But even for that segment of the organizations in the world for whom a private cloud might makes sense from a size perspective, there's another argument against building private clouds: what business are you in? Are you in the datacenter business? Do your revenues come from building a bigger and better data infrastructure than anyone else or does that give you a competitive advantage? If not, why do it? Why not spend your money and effort on innovating your core business rather than investing in what will only be another cost center? And, along with that argument is the one that you would not have access to many of the tools that make the cloud so effective—for example, object stores. You would be stuck in the previous generation of cloud technology, and thus behind your competition, instead of being on the leading edge.

So, all in all, it rarely, if ever, makes sense to build a private cloud specially for data platforms.

Data Platforms for Data 2.0

Data 2.0 is all about building data lakes in the cloud and using the data platforms built for the cloud to drive agility and a self-service data culture.

The significant benefits that the cloud provides for building a data-driven culture are increasingly driving the emergence and adoption of data platforms built for the cloud. Whereas Data 1.0 was based on datacenter computing and creating data lake architectures on-premises, Data 2.0 is all about building data lakes in the cloud and using the data platforms built for the cloud to drive agility and a self-service data culture.

The Facebooks and Googles of the world were visionary companies that already had significant big data investments and had the ability to begin to construct some of these platforms tools that they designed and built themselves. However, this is a very complex task, something beyond the capabilities of most companies. Still, there are other ways for most businesses to reach Data 2.0 status. In the cloud, data platforms can be used as a service. They do not need to be consumed in the form of software or an open source distribution—mechanisms that were the norm for Data 1.0. The as-a-service model means that the complexities of building data platforms out of open source distributions or software and the significant need for specialized expertise that they require are a thing of the past. Through the as-a-service model, enterprises can now reach the same "nirvana" stage that has so far been attainable only by the likes of Facebook and Google. Through the as-a-service model of Data 2.0, the data teams of these enterprises can become the catalysts for ushering in the data culture and therefore, transforming their respective companies.

Data 2.0 uses the cloud and data platform as-a-service model to make companies data-driven. Whereas the Data 1.0 approach of the past takes months and years to build and propagate a data-driven culture, Data 2.0 helps data teams usher in that transformation in weeks.

Summary

Big data and data platforms are increasingly vital for businesses. To create a data-driven culture, the agility and flexibility of these platforms are very important. Cloud architecture with its scalability, elasticity, usage tracking, and cost savings is the best infrastructure on which to build and deploy these data platforms. The cloud's separation of compute and storage, security architecture, and scalable object stores are important capabilities that Data 2.0 platforms need to build on, in order to enable data teams to reach the "nirvana" of the data-driven culture in their companies.

CHAPTER 7

Metadata and Big Data

Data by itself means very little. After all, a piece of digital data is simply a collection of bits. To be discovered (found) or understood, this collection of bits needs something called *metadata*. In this chapter, we cover what metadata is and why it's important to the self-service data model.

First, a basic definition: metadata is any information that gives you information about the data. It's data about data.

The Three Types of Metadata

There are different kinds of metadata that describe different aspects of the data with which they are associated. Specifically, metadata can be categorized as one of three types: descriptive, structural, or administrative, as illustrated in Figure 7-1.

Depending on the type of metadata, it is used for different purposes. For example, descriptive metadata would be used when business analysts want to know what exactly the data consists of. Structural metadata would tell us the relationship between different datasets. And administrative metadata would inform us about ownership and rights management.

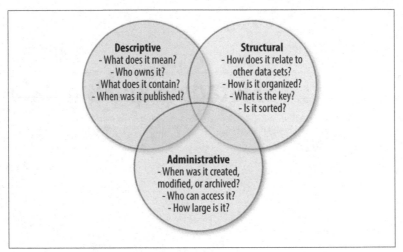

Figure 7-1. Classes of metadata

Descriptive Metadata

Descriptive metadata describes a collection of bits, or piece of digital data, so that it can be cataloged, discovered, identified, explored, and so on. It can include elements such as title, abstract, author, and keywords. It is typically meant to be read by humans.

Descriptive metadata can also help data users "decode" data. For example, suppose that you've administered a survey to a number of users, and have captured their answers to the multiple-choice survey as one of five letters: a, b, c, d, and e. Although the data itself might consist only of the letters, the descriptive metadata informs you how to interpret those letters. The single most important attribute of descriptive metadata is that it allows data users to understand what the data is, and how to use it.

In addition to direct applications for data users, this type of metadata is also used by data discovery tools to aid the data users in finding, exploring, and understanding datasets.

Structural Metadata

Structural metadata is data about the organization of information and the relationship between different organizational units. It informs either the data users or machines about how the data is organized so that they can perform transformations on it and correlate it with other datasets. Among other aspects of data, structural metadata describes the types, versions, relationships, and other characteristics of digital data.

For example, structural metadata could consist of specifying the different types of columns in a table, or how to interpret a comma-separated values (CSV) file using a processing engine like SQL. It could capture information about foreign key relationships between two datasets, whether some parts of the datasets are unique keys or whether the data is time partitioned. These are just some examples of characteristics about data that can be captured by structural metadata.

This structural information is primarily put in place to make the data actionable, whether it be by machines using data processing engines or by data users using different types of query languages. It can be used by software to choose optimal computation paths for the desired transformation so that the results can be provided as quickly as possible. As an example, simple information on whether a dataset is sorted or not can be used to choose techniques that can avoid inspecting all data values while searching for a specific value.

Administrative Metadata

Administrative metadata provides information to help administrators manage a resource, such as when and how it was created, file type, who can access it, and other technical information. It captures information during the entire lifecycle of data, from creation, through consumption, through changes, and then finally to archival or deletion. The information is most easily captured by software aiding in all of these activities. Given this information, one of the key applications of administrative data is compliance and auditing.

Another part of administrative data captures organizational policies related to data management. Such policies might be specified to control any or all aspects the lifecycle of data. As an example, a key policy element around data that every organization deals with is controlling access to it. Access control lists (ACLs) and permissions are elements of administrative metadata that help administrators with managing access to different part of the data's lifecycle—creation, consumption (read), modification (update), deletion of archival. Another example of a policy element associated with data management could be specifications of the duration of time when data is held online and when it is either deleted or archived away.

These policies could also dictate how and in where the different durations are stored and managed.

As is evident, administrators' administrative tools are heavy users of administrative metadata to manage data. Data users do not use it as much.

The Challenges of Metadata

One of the biggest challenge with metadata is consistency: what are the processes for creating, modifying, and managing the metadata?

Metadata is essential for creating a self-service data infrastructure. If the descriptive metadata is not available for a dataset, business users and analysts won't be able to identify it and will continually go to the experts—the central data team—for help. This obviously would defeat the purpose of having a self-service data infrastructure.

Similarly, if administrative metadata is not available, issues of access control, security, and data quality would go unresolved. Data quality is an especially important reason to have a well-managed administrative metadata. If the quality of data is not good, no one will use it, or if they do use it, they will arrive at the wrong conclusions.

One of the biggest challenges with metadata is *consistency*: what are the processes for creating, modifying, and managing the metadata? Analysis depends on independent datasets. Independency means that the datasets are collecting different characteristics of a particular entity. Independent datasets very often are created by different applications, teams, and, many times, by different organizations. Clearly, in such a federated authoring process, without any standards, different publishers would describe or structure the data sets in a different way. As a result, metadata about the data from these different sources diverges.

As a simple example, take the case of datasets that collect the postal address of a set of entities in the United States. In some datasets, the postal address might be captured in six different, highly structured fields that capture the street number, the street name, the suite number, the city, the state, and the zip code. On the other hand, in other datasets the postal address could be captured simply through free form text field. Note that the structural metadata for the postal address in these two datasets is different. Consequently, data users trying to correlate the postal address field in the two datasets would have the unenviable task of figuring out how to do it. They would need to inspect the data carefully or ask someone knowledgeable. Both of those actions would eat up valuable time.

So, the standards for creating and managing metadata within an organization and many times within an industry are very important. And, equally important, after the standards are in place, how do you ensure that they are adhered to? At times, there is no control over the metadata about certain datasets. In such situations, it becomes important to find ways and mechanisms of "merging" the metadata from the different sources. There are other challenges with metadata, as well, including the high cost of creating and managing it and figuring out what the exact value of doing so is to the organization.

Effectively Managing Metadata

Metadata management is a key responsibility of the data team within an organization. This certainly applies to the datasets that it is publishing to the rest of the organization. For the derivative datasets, the team can act as a source of best practices or providers of tools that help the data users to create compliant metadata for their own datasets.

Broadly speaking, organizations can choose from a spectrum of approaches to metadata management. At one end of the spectrum are tightly coupled, highly centralized approaches, and at the other end are loosely coupled, decentralized approaches to metadata management. Let's take a look at each of these approaches:

Make metadata creation and management extremely regimented and controlled
> With most data warehouses, this was the approach taken. Metadata standards would be published, and everyone dealing with that data warehouse would adhere to the mandated naming conventions. If anything changed, the metadata would also be changed in a very structured way using metadata management (MDM) tools. This very centralized process put a heavy emphasis on change management processes. The advantage: data and metadata would always be in sync, and there would be no ambiguity or inconsistency in how the metadata was created and managed. The disadvantage: this process is not necessarily agile and at times might be difficult to enforce on datasets coming

from third-party organizations. Especially in the latter case, this approach to metadata management would stipulate that the dataset had to go through a "conversion" process in order to be compliant with the metadata rules of the organization.

"Crowdsource" metadata management
Using tools—either commercial, or home-grown—some organizations have taken a "wiki" approach to metadata. Using this approach, any user can create or edit metadata. The advantage of this approach: you capture the knowledge and capabilities of the crowd, not just maintain the status quo of existing standards. This approach is also agile and flexible. The disadvantage of this approach: it needs a critical mass of users invested in maintaining it in order to be effective.

The right approach to metadata differs from organization to organization. The right approach can also be a combination of these two approaches with a higher dependence on one versus another depending on the needs and the culture of the organization.

At Facebook, we originally took the first approach: everything was highly controlled. Then, we went to the crowdsourced model because that was more in tune with the agility and flexibility of a fast-growing organization that believed in a decentralized self-service culture. Then, we eventually migrated to an approach that was somewhere between the two extremes by using software automation.

As part of this initiative, we built intelligent software to aid metadata creation, curation, and maintenance. To begin, we built portals that encouraged users to fill out standard fields—sometimes software intelligence would be prefilled with information derived from the data. Part of this portal would also give recognition to the users who were contributing and maintaining metadata—these users would be recognized as experts for those datasets. In addition, the software suite would use this metadata in innovative ways to make data discovery, job authoring, debugging, and tuning easier for users. A number of these innovations were rolled into the portal.

At Facebook, taking a "middle" approach was really the best of both worlds. We used accepted naming conventions, yet we could use the wisdom of the crowd to generate descriptive metadata. This way, we were not constricted by existing standards, yet we also did not create a digital Tower of Babel. We got the power of software automation, and intelligence in the metadata without the rigidity. Ultimately, the middle approach yielded a very robust metadata set for us, which was important to self-service data infrastructure.

Summary

Creating and managing metadata effectively and efficiently is essential for a self-service data infrastructure. Without accurate and consistent metadata, your datasets will not be as useful as they otherwise would be, and your users will constantly be running to the data team for clarification on the metadata. Instituting a "middle of the road" metadata management philosophy using standards, crowdsourcing, and software automation will help you achieve metadata that is both accurate and relevant.

CHAPTER 8

A Maturity-Model "Reality Check" for Organizations

Chapter 2 discussed Qubole's five-step data maturity model, but how does that model align with what companies are really doing? Are companies actually maturing along this spectrum as expected? Where are most companies now? More important, how does *your* organization fit into the model, and how does its maturity affect your ability to make data-driven decisions?

To find out what organizations were actually doing with their big data initiatives, Qubole commissioned a global survey of 406 senior executives from organizations across a range of industries. The primary research goal was to capture the status of big data projects within enterprise companies, and to answer the questions of "where are people today?" and "where do people want to be?" while shedding light on some of the challenges that they will face getting there.

Organizations Understand the Need for Big Data, But Reach Is Still Limited

Big data is still a very limited deployment.

Upon reviewing the survey results, the first insight we had was that virtually every organization today hopes to take advantage of big data. Only four percent of organizations surveyed said that attempting to harness big data didn't make sense for their business. Equal proportions of companies said they have been using big data for some time (38 percent) or were just getting started on big data projects (38 percent). Although the remaining 20 percent don't currently have big data projects in place, they expect to in the future (Figure 8-1).

This tells us that the notion that everyone should be making use of big data is both well understood and widely accepted.

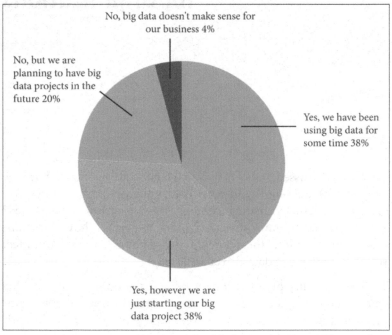

No, big data doesn't make sense for our business 4%

No, but we are planning to have big data projects in the future 20%

Yes, we have been using big data for some time 38%

Yes, however we are just starting our big data project 38%

Figure 8-1. Does your company currently have a big data initiative? (Source: The State of Data Ops—A Global Survey of IT and Data Professionals, February 2017, Dimensional Research)

Despite this broad interest in big data, it seems that big data activity has yet to reach deeply into most organizations. Less than half of respondents (45 percent) say they are seeing more than four groups requesting big data projects today (Figure 8-2).

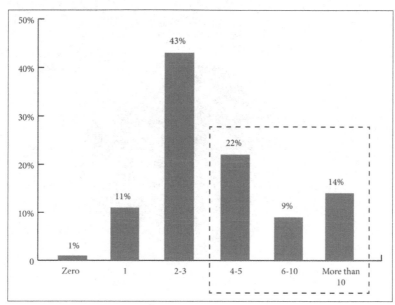

Figure 8-2. How many different groups are requesting big data projects today? (Source: The State of Data Ops—A Global Survey of IT and Data Professionals, February 2017, Dimensional Research)

What this tells us is that big data is still a very limited deployment. Enthusiasm for taking advantage of data and analytics hasn't spread throughout most organizations. Yet our core theory behind writing this book is that every company should want to provide ubiquitous access to data and analytics to all of their users to become fully data-driven. If all employees in a company have this kind of access, they will be able to do their jobs better and be more competitive and efficient while reducing costs.

If you look back at the illustration of Qubole's data maturity model in Chapter 2, you'll see that most organizations are at Stage 2 or Stage 3.

Reinforcing these conclusions, when asked to assess themselves, 88 percent of respondents said they were still in the early stages of big data adoption (Figure 8-3).

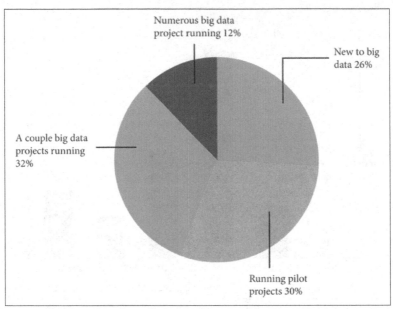

Figure 8-3. Where is your company in terms of adopting big data? (Source: The State of Data Ops—A Global Survey of IT and Data Professionals, February 2017, Dimensional Research)

As would follow by their self-assessments, very few respondents say they have full mature processes that provide tools and access to insights for all stakeholders. Only eight percent rated themselves as having this capability—they are the only ones who have reached Stage 5 (Nirvana) in Qubole's maturity model. Another seven percent say they have proven processes, but still can't meet business demand. These are organizations at Stage 4 that are in the process of figuring out how to make self-service work, but have yet to make it all work together. This means that only 15 percent aggregate have mature self-service processes (Figure 8-4).

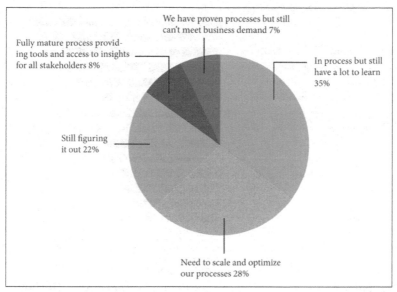

Figure 8-4. How do you assess your big data maturity? (Source: The State of Data Ops—A Global Survey of IT and Data Professionals, February 2017, Dimensional Research)

Significant Challenges Remain

A full 93 percent of respondents say that demand for big data analyses is growing. Meeting that demand is impossible without moving to a self-service model.

We found that 98 percent of organizations are facing a significant array of challenges. The foremost challenge? Data quality, with almost half of respondents (48 percent) saying that was a problem for them (Figure 8-5). The cost and measurable value of big data projects were also concerns (46 percent and 40 percent, respectively). Satisfying the needs of business users also came out in the top five concerns (45 percent).

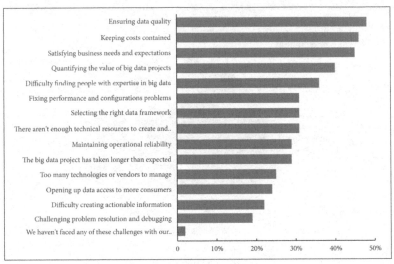

Figure 8-5. Big data challenges (Source: The State of Data Ops—A Global Survey of IT and Data Professionals, February 2017, Dimensional Research)

Although it is useful to see which challenges came out on top, the clustering of these challenges at very close percentages tells us that most companies are facing *many* challenges, and that the key takeaway is that big data is difficult and complex, and presents many obstacles to harnessing it adequately.

What Figure 8-5 also tells us is that, again, most organizations aren't that far along in reaching a self-service data culture. Demand is growing for access to data by employees, but the ability of the data team to meet that demand is still stymied by these challenges.

One of the main points of this book is that we want organizations to understand that if they continue to run IT as a service function, they'll never achieve big data Nirvana. Until IT reinvents itself to be an enabler of self-service, no organization will achieve the goal of ubiquitous access. The business will always want more than IT is able to give. An interesting observation that we often make is that big data is very complex, and has no "leverage." By this we mean that the more you get closer to ubiquitous access, the harder it becomes to fulfill the user's expectations. Transitioning your model to self-service is the only way to get there.

This lack of leverage applies to cost, as well. Cost increases disproportionately as the scale of your big data increases. And this can be very difficult to quantify from a business perspective.

One of the reasons for this is the way that most organizations commence with their big data projects. As you'll see from a later question, most organizations begin by building their big data infrastructure on-premises. That means they have to buy a number of costly servers, deploy them in their datacenters with the appropriate software, and test it all together. This process alone can take months or even years—and that's before you get to run your first query. So, you're perhaps 13 or 15 months into a big data project, and you're finally ready to ask your first question. You haven't even encountered any of the operational challenges yet. If you were asked at that point for your return on investment (ROI), you simply wouldn't have any idea.

Additionally, you need to make a large investment to quantify the ROI. But the quandary most companies find themselves in is how do they make large investments if they can't quantify the ROI? It's a chicken-or-egg problem.

The cloud has changed the scenario dramatically. You still have quite a few organizations that invested in on-premises big data infrastructure, but increasingly, the number of companies that weren't willing to make that kind of investment or quickly realized that cloud was a better option are building their big data infrastructure in the cloud.

The survey revealed that companies are also having trouble finding big data expertise (36 percent of respondents). A full two-thirds of them are being forced to depend on third-party consulting resources to deploy and manage their big data initiatives.

Figure 8-6 reinforces the fact that data teams are fighting challenges on multiple fronts. In the figure, you see that although performance is the number one goal for operational improvements (56 percent) among these big data teams, it is followed so closely by data quality (54 percent) and automation (52 percent) that it's clear data teams are besieged on all sides. In effect, Figure 8-6 underscores the fact that having the data team act like a service organization quickly becomes the bottleneck for a big data initiative.

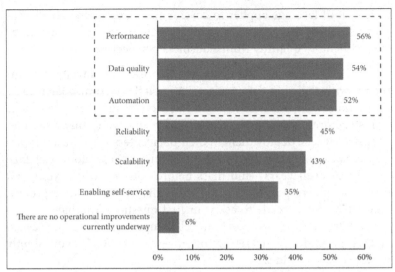

Figure 8-6. Which of the following is the data team currently working to improve? (Source: The State of Data Ops—A Global Survey of IT and Data Professionals, February 2017, Dimensional Research)

To stress this point, Figure 8-7 informs us that a full 93 percent of respondents say that demand for big data analyses is growing. Meeting that demand is impossible without moving to a self-service model.

Despite this, more than three-fourths of respondents (78%) said they still respond to requests for big data initiatives on a project-by-project basis. Only 22 percent say they have achieved a true self-service model.

Yet, oddly enough, the majority of companies (64 percent) say they want to achieve self-service and have concrete plans in place to do so. In fact, 87 percent of companies *are confident* that they can provide self-service analytics when the time is right (Figure 8-8).

As Chapter 2 mentions, the pivotal point in the maturity model is when organizations attempt to move from Stage 3 to Stage 4. Many organizations experience a moment of truth when they realize that they will never get there without transitioning to a self-service model. Their big data initiatives might be expanding, and they might think they are making progress, but inevitably they will hit this roadblock.

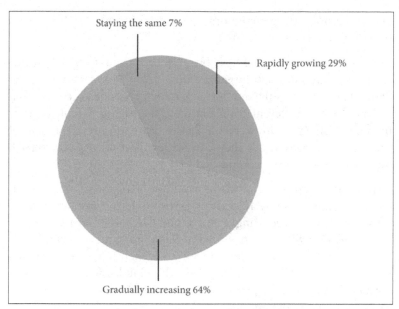

Figure 8-7. How is the business's demand for big data anlysis changing? (Source: The State of Data Ops—A Global Survey of IT and Data Professionals, February 2017, Dimensional Research)

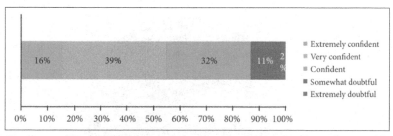

Figure 8-8. How confident are you that the data team can achieve self-service analytics? (Source: The State of Data Ops—A Global Survey of IT and Data Professionals, February 2017, Dimensional Research)

For us, the takeaway of Figure 8-8 is that companies are underestimating the difficulty of this transition to a self-service data model. This reminds us of a few years ago, when companies were convinced that they could build their own private clouds—that they could do better than the public cloud vendors. They eventually had to admit that their private clouds would never be as big, as cheap, as scalable, reliable, or secure as an Amazon or Microsoft public cloud. So, even if they succeeded in building a private cloud, they had effectively fallen behind their competitors who simply used a public cloud from the beginning.

This suggests that there's a little bit of hubris around big data infrastructure. But although organizations might think they've been doing data warehousing and business intelligence for years, and that it won't be that different from big data, the reality is that it's a lot more difficult. How do we reconcile the fact that only 13 percent of organizations don't think they can achieve self-service, yet only 8 percent have actually accomplished it?

Organizations around the world are bullish on the cloud when it comes to big data. Only 12 percent of respondents reject any idea of putting big data processing in the cloud. Although 30 percent say they aren't doing it now, they reserve the opportunity to do it in the future. And the rest do either some or all of their big data processing in the cloud. As Chapter 6 observes, the cloud offers tremendous advantages for big data processing, including scalability and elasticity among others (Figure 8-9).

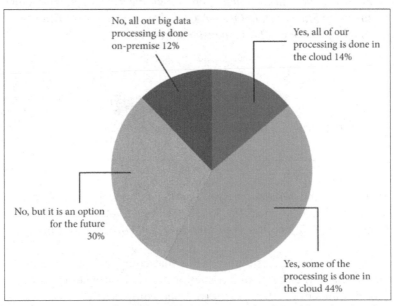

Figure 8-9. Is any of your big data processing performed in the cloud? (Source: The State of Data Ops—A Global Survey of IT and Data Professionals, February 2017, Dimensional Research)

As we pointed out, organizations are moving their workloads to the cloud. A full 96 percent of companies have at least part of their big data infrastructure in the cloud. A little more than half (54 percent) have at least part on-premises. Yet, for all the reasons we've given in this chapter, we believe that more and more organizations will commit to the cloud for big data (Figure 8-10).

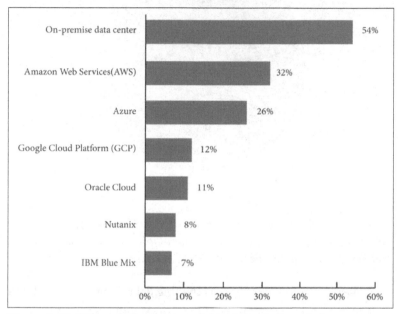

Figure 8-10. Where is the company's big data platform infrastructure located? (Source: The State of Data Ops—A Global Survey of IT and Data Professionals, February 2017, Dimensional Research)

Although 78 percent of companies are at some stage of planning or deploying a big data platform, only 19 percent have a platform fully deployed and in use. Only three percent of respondents do not plan to deploy a big data platform (Figure 8-11). This ties back to the question about challenges, and why so many organizations are having trouble quantifying the ROI of big data initiatives. With less than one in five organizations having a fully deployed platform, it shouldn't be surprising that most organizations can't prove ROI. A full 73 percent of respondents are simply not at a place where they can even consider trying to calculate ROI.

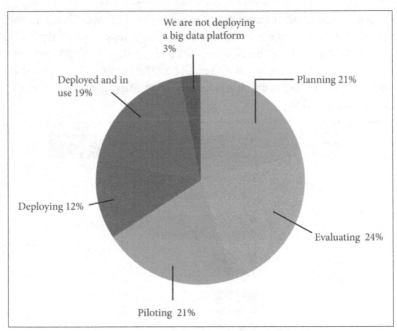

Figure 8-11. Where is your company with respect to deploying a big data platform? (Source: The State of Data Ops—A Global Survey of IT and Data Professionals, February 2017, Dimensional Research)

The takeaway from Figure 8-12 is that big data is made up of a lot of diverse workloads. Therefore, you need a "complete" platform to handle all of them—a platform that supports different transformation engines and tools for different workloads and user personas. In addition, making this platform self-service and meeting the diverse needs of multiple workloads and users becomes an increasingly difficult task.

Application data integration leads the current big data workloads (53 percent), followed by ad hoc analytics (41 percent), and ETL (37 percent).

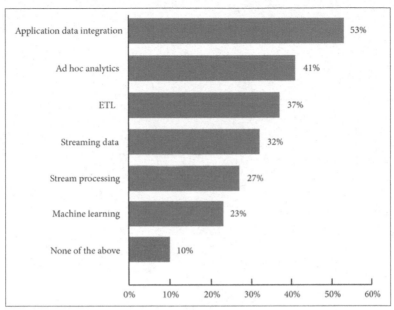

Figure 8-12. Is the data team currently supporting any of these work-loads? (Source: The State of Data Ops—A Global Survey of IT and Data Professionals, February 2017, Dimensional Research)

Summary

In summary, most companies today are still in the early stages of moving to a self-service infrastructure that can fully support their big data aspirations. Most would be at either Stage 1 or Stage 2 of the Qubole Data-Driven Maturity Model. Although on one level they seem cognizant of this fact, in other ways they appear to have unrealistic expectations of exactly how much effort and expertise it will require for them to progress to the next maturity stage. This appears to be a case where the more they learn, the more realistic and tempered their expectations and goals will be.

PART II
Case Studies

In Part II, we present four case studies contributed by data professionals at leading companies at different stages of the self-service journey.

In Chapter 9, we get some insight from LinkedIn. As with all consumer web companies, there has always been an enormous amount of data that's flowed through LinkedIn. But the organization was relatively early to realize the importance of this data. This chapter shows how by centralizing a data group and creating a self-service infrastructure, employees throughout LinkedIn began making data-driven decisions.

In Chapter 10, we learn about Uber. The company realized that the only way to ensure that it could offer good user experience with operational efficiency was by using data effectively. Uber's challenge was that it was too successful—growing too fast to have a coherent plan. This chapter explains how the company adapted and changed its data strategy to accommodate that growth.

Chapter 11 profiles Twitter, an organization that is all about real time and that needs infrastructure to handle data in real time to do analytics and provide insights. The company built Heron, a real-time, distributed, and fault-tolerant stream-processing engine that has powered all of Twitter's real-time analytics across since 2014.

Looking ahead, Twitter is hoping to build a system that can identify and fix problems as they are occurring.

Finally, in Chapter 12, we look at eBay. From its early days, eBay had a strong data-driven culture and strong executive support for data initiatives, recognizing how important they were to the company. eBay had long been tracking "transactional" data, but it had just been throwing out very important "behavioral" data about its customers. In this case study, we see how eBay learned to capture and analyze all of its data to drive the daily decision-making processes of the company, and how it built a self-service big data infrastructure to support all of this data and analytics.

CHAPTER 9

LinkedIn: The Road to Data Craftsmanship

by Shrikanth Shankar, director of engineering, analytical platforms, and apps at LinkedIn

I've been with LinkedIn for only 18 months. Yet, what I've seen in data operations has amazed me. Like all consumer web companies, there's always been an enormous amount of data that's flowed through LinkedIn. But LinkedIn was relatively early to realize the importance of this data.

At LinkedIn, it wasn't just about getting the analytics right. The company realized early on that infrastructure had to go hand in hand with analytics to support the data ecosystem. Many open source projects, most famously Apache Kafka, were born at LinkedIn to support this ecosystem. Today at LinkedIn, we rely heavily on the scalability and reliability of Kafka, Hadoop, and a surrounding ecosystem of open source and internally developed tools to serve our analytic needs.

Early on, the company found that different teams—such as the Email Team, and the Homepage Team—were using disparate tools when building data pipelines, as illustrated in Figure 9-1.

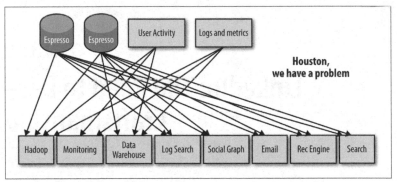

Figure 9-1. Different teams built and operated different pipelines (source: LinkedIn)[1]

LinkedIn knew, of course, that it shouldn't have multiple pipelines for moving and ingesting data, or for computing metrics. It's inefficient and difficult to manage, and, most important, it leads to inconsistent and unpredictable results because many things (e.g., how users are tracked, schemas, and application layout) change all the time. Metrics could then become incorrect because the logic would not be updated to deal with these changes.

To unify its data ecosystem, LinkedIn first built a unified transport pipeline using Kafka, as demonstrated in Figure 9-2.

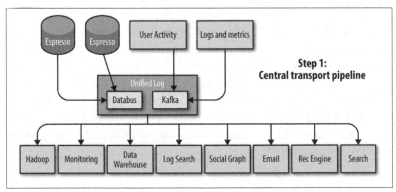

Figure 9-2. Creating a central transport pipeline using Kafka (source: LinkedIn)

---

1 Bigger, Faster, Easier—LinkedIn Hadoop Summit 2015 (*https://www.slideshare.net/Shir shankaDas/linkedin-49299589*)

Then, LinkedIn built a central ingestion framework that allowed it to remove all of the custom jobs that were ingesting this data into Hadoop (see Figure 9-3). This removed the burden of managing and monitoring multiple custom pipelines and moved the work to a unified service built using Gobblin, LinkedIn's open source ingestion framework.

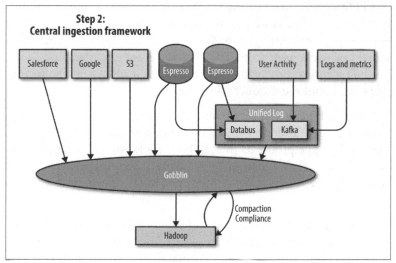

Figure 9-3. Creating a unified ingestion framework (source: LinkedIn)

The next step was to unify the metric computation. When I arrived, the team was working on the second generation of a unified platform for computing metrics. We were moving beyond using this platform for experimentation to supporting reporting and other analytics use cases. This centralized platform allowed us to impose governance and quality controls on the data. There was now just one place to go to edit the logic, so if product analysts wanted to change something, there was no confusion about where the logic was, who it affected, or the process for changing it.

Now, we have a way for analysts, data scientists, and engineers to define metrics using the language of their choice, whether it's Hive, Pig, or something else. A significant percentage of these metrics can be expressed declaratively, which allows the data infrastructure team to keep adding more execution platforms and optimizations. The platform code generates the entire flow, and we push all these computed metrics into a distributed Online Analytical Processing (OLAP) engine called Pinot that we also built here.

The platform handles a lot of the features that we need in metrics, such as computing them incrementally, aggregating them, and back-filling them.

Tracking and DALI

Tracking is a big part of the LinkedIn ecosystem. Metrics are ultimately only as reliable as the data that generates them. Various applications are continuously dropping "breadcrumbs" about what individual users have done. That's what we use to understand how a product is doing, how people are using it, and then to make further decisions about the product's direction.

When we adopted a new tracking methodology, we knew that things would change. Producers would be constantly making changes to it. One of the huge problems that we had was keeping data consumers isolated from these changes. If I add a column, does that break somebody else's script because they don't know how to deal with this new column?

So, in 2015, we built DALI, a data abstraction layer that enables producers to create new versions of data while allowing consumers of the data to keep using the versions that they have without having to deal with any changes. DALI hid details from users about how data was produced. Users would simply get a pageview event. They could use that even as producers continued changing the definition of the pageview event. DALI also allowed us to hide details of physical location, format, and so on from users.

This functionality proved to be a huge win for us when we launched Voyager, a new mobile version of LinkedIn. That's what allowed us to consistently have insights into what was happening with the product.

Faster Access to Data and Insights

Another significant data-driven initiative at LinkedIn is to make data available much more quickly. You need to be deliberate about these things because these metrics are used for things like A/B testing. And when you are doing A/B testing, you need sufficient data to make determinations. LinkedIn will typically look at a entire day's worth of data before it flags a metric. But we are getting to the stage when—as you ship faster and faster—you need quicker insights into what's happening on the product site.

We didn't want a data world in which there was one pipeline that was computing the daily metrics and another pipeline that was computing hourly metrics. So, we extended our centralized metrics platform such that that users could just flip a configuration and the metric would show up on an hourly schedule. This gave us much faster insights without losing the benefits of centralization and governance. With this new platform, within two hours of something happening, you'd have an understanding of how a new feature was doing in terms of impact on users.

This platform powers multiple ecosystems. As already discussed, the A/B testing platform was one of the big consumers of this data. We also built a dashboard tool called "Raptor" that allows people to visualize these metrics. Finally, we built an anomaly detection and monitoring tool that quickly exposes problems and tries to identify the root cause for metric drops.

Organizational Structure of the Data Team

We want more people to do more things with the data. But at the same time, when we make decisions, we want to make sure that that data we are using is clean and correct.

At LinkedIn, like most data-driven companies, we have a centralized data team. Then, within that team, there are subgroups in charge of different data activities. For example, we have a team that focuses on tracking. They look at questions such as how to track users and their behavior across the entire ecosystem, in a sensible fashion. What's the right way? What sort of events should we be tracking?"

Then we have a team that focuses on A/B testing, which is largely made up of data scientists. A/B testing is very data science–heavy and you want expert statisticians on that team.

A separate analytics team works very closely with the product engineering and the product management teams on defining the necessary metrics, such as the precise definition of a pageview. The definition is important because that defines the metrics we use for making decisions.

Then, there are product managers who set product direction and are also responsible for running the A/B experiments and making decisions about whether the experiments are working. The experimentation team works with them to use data to determine if an experiment actually improved or hurt key business metrics like pageviews.

A central hub of analysts works closely with the product teams. They create the metrics by defining the logic on UMP, but then product managers are provided with dashboard tools to query and get their questions answered.

We also built executive dashboards that are produced by a centralized reporting team and then shared with executives and other consumers.

We are constantly struggling with the fact that we want more people to do more things with the data. But at the same time, when we make decisions, we want to ensure that the data we are using is clean and correct. That's something we're constantly thinking about—how do we balance those things?

The Move to Self-Service

To democratize data even more, we've been working on making the data access and analysis tools simpler to use.

One of the moves we made in 2016 was to give each team access to a subset of the company's Hadoop resources. At that point, people began using the data in a self-service manner. They also began self-policing because they were conscious that their team had a limited quota of resources. Today, if people know that someone on their team is running a very expensive script without sufficient justification, they talk to them. In effect, the teams set up their own usage controls.

To democratize data even more, we've been working on making the data access and analysis tools simpler to use. On the older ecosystem, users had Tableau; on the modern data stack, many of these tools are still works in progress. Raptor, our home-grown tool for dashboarding, is the most popular.

Future plans include developing more user-friendly tools. Today, the analytics team does their data prep work—getting the metrics definitions ready, and so on—and then people are able to slice and dice that fairly easily. But then if they want to take that same dataset and join it with another dataset, there's no simple way to do any of that.

Our internal tools today don't support that. That's something we'd like to look at.

Data has helped us be very deliberate about the product decisions we make. We have significantly more insight into how our products are doing and what the impact of a product adjustment would be, before making any big changes. And I think that gives people a way to balance their instincts.

CHAPTER 10

Uber: Driven to Democratize Data

by Zheng Shao, software engineer at Uber

As a company, Uber's mission is to make transportation as reliable as running water. To achieve this, we need to provide a seamless user experience for both riders and drivers as well as be operationally efficient. Both of these goals require the highly proficient and effective use of data.

Data is key to managing supply and demand on our platform. For instance, data enables us to connect drivers with nearby riders to optimize routes for distance and time, maximizing the amount of money made by drivers and reducing the amount of time waited by riders after requesting a trip. Improving the performance of our driver/rider network also means more efficient carpooling with uberPOOL, allowing riders to share rides and save money. Because many factors affect the efficiency of carpooling, data helps us identify the best rider-driver route combinations. For both drivers and riders, data-based optimization is critical for a seamless Uber experience.

Fueled by our data-driven decisions, Uber is a technology company focused on creating new innovations that help improve transportation. It's crucially important to democratize data so that teams at Uber can utilize it well, regardless of their level of technical skills.

Uber's First Data Challenge: Too Popular

One of the first challenges Uber had was that it was growing so fast, and teams were scrambling to keep up with this growth. Every team tried to do its own data analysis, and soon each had its own data-driven processes, which resulted in inconsistent data across teams.

So, Uber's first step toward data democratization was to establish a centralized data organization that would be responsible for the company-wide data platform. This centralized team is important for two reasons: consistency and efficiency. The first, consistency, is obvious. We can't have two different teams define the same driver rating average value with different formula (for example, moving average and lifetime average). If one team found drivers getting an average rating of 4.8, and another 4.6, that would make our data confusing to internal users.

The second reason for centralizing our data team is efficiency. The bigger the data is, the costlier it will be. We need to handle our data efficiently to minimize those costs. Increasing granularity gives us more insights but increases the cost because more hardware will be needed. A centralized team also makes centralized access control for compliance, privacy, and security more efficient.

Uber's Second Data Challenge: Scalability

The next step toward achieving a data democratization was to build a centralized data organization that could *scale*. This was difficult because the demand for data outgrew what the earlier data team could support, on both the people side and the technology side.

Within Uber, there is a lot of interest from all levels of the organization in utilizing data, meaning that every engineer on the data team is always extremely busy. This inundation of requests for data can be overwhelming, and it's important to hire people with the skills necessary to deal with this grueling workflow. In fact, hiring the right people to put in place a sound organizational structure, the efficient processes, and the necessary amount of automation is a deal breaker when determining the success of the data team.

The second scaling challenge relates to choosing—and building—the right types of technologies to keep up with Uber's hyper-growth. In 2015, the company adopted a lot of open source big data technologies. In general, open source technologies are widely used in the industry and are therefore more battle-tested for a variety of workloads and scalabilities.

Hiring to Scale: Six Roles to Fill

The first consideration when hiring to scale is to identify the roles for which you need to hire. Although small companies might consider hiring only generalists, larger companies like Uber work with systems that can become very niche and complex. In the latter case, it makes much more sense to hire specialists to round out the team. Larger companies need to hire a lot of specialists, from the customer-facing level (product managers) to the infrastructure-facing level (site reliability engineers). To effectively scale our data team at Uber, we looked to fill the following six roles:

Product managers
> People in this role define the metrics and think about how data as a product interacts with multiple different teams inside the company.

Data scientists
> Data scientists, usually statisticians or machine-learning experts, must make sense of the numbers—not just to analyze existing data, but to predict the future using data. If we can predict when and how many riders will be calling Uber at what place and at what point in time, we can direct drivers to go to those places even before the rider requests an Uber. That is really powerful because it can substantially reduce the amount of time a rider must wait to be picked up. This is not just a dream—it's already happening to some degree. For example, as is to be expected, weekday mornings at urban train stations is a popular time and location for ride requests. These are historical patterns that Uber can take advantage of to predict demand and improve the efficiency of the service.

Data engineers
> (Some companies call them data architects.) These are the professionals who understand the semantics of the data and business logic. These engineers define concepts like daily actives, monthly actives, and so on and how those different concepts relate to one another. Data engineers transform raw datasets to produce what we call modeled datasets. These modeled datasets are very powerful because they allow people like data scientists and product managers to more easily analyze the data. The modeled datasets also allow data scientists and product manag-

ers to access the data much more efficiently, making their data clusters more efficient.

Data product engineers
These individuals focus on the entire lifecycle of the data and its users. For example, data scientists can create machine learning models to improve Uber's products, but after they put the improvements in place, they will need to fine-tune their evolutionary model again, to improve their results. This entire workflow can be standardized via an internal product, and that's why we have data product engineers.

Data infrastructure engineers
People in this role need to be very familiar with the big data ecosystem, understand both open source software and proprietary big data software, and the pros and cons of each. They need to be very well connected within the community as well as understand new trends in technology, problems with existing technologies, and what technologies other companies are using. Data infrastructure engineers ensure that we don't do everything from scratch, but instead blend open source software with home-grown solutions to support the unique business needs in an efficient manner. At the same time, we contribute commonly used features back to the open source community. In that way, we foster very collaborative relationships with other companies for the betterment of the industry.

Site reliability engineers
Similar in function to a DevOps engineer, this role was introduced by Google. This professional automates the management of large-scale clusters and sets the bar for production quality and reliability, making it more efficient to manage huge data clusters without having to worry about hardware failures.

Technical Scalability

Uber's initial data stack included massively parallel processing (MPP) architecture that used proprietary technology. MPP is traditionally more efficient in a small-scale cluster because it assigns each node to a specific function. For example, if we have 10 nodes, we can divide the job into 10 pieces, so each node will take exactly 10 percent of the work. This approach is centrally organized and typically results in high efficiency when everything runs smoothly. However, things become trickier if you have 1,000 machines and each of the machines is responsible for 0.1 percent of the work. From a purely statistical perspective, the likelihood that any one machine inside this cluster experiences an issue is high, and in reality, this can happen every day, at any time. Sometimes, these issues are hardware-related, but most frequently they're software-related. Ultimately, when the machines in a cluster are no longer performing equally fast, the MPP architecture determines that the efficiency of the cluster will be based on the slowest node, and all the other, faster machines must move at the pace of the slowest node. As a result, the efficiency of this architecture decreases as the cluster grows.

In 2004, Google published a paper on a new approach called Map-Reduce (*https://research.google.com/archive/mapreduce-osdi04.pdf*). Map-Reduce differs from MPP in that it distributes work across all the nodes in a very different way. In Map-Reduce, whichever node finishes the work first can be assigned more work; this means that the entire cluster can take advantage of the faster nodes, while the slower nodes run less work. Ultimately, the job is completed by taking the full capability of every single node in the cluster.

Although this approach might be a little less efficient than MPP when every machine works perfectly well, it offers greater speed and scalability in case of failures. As an example, Hadoop was based on this architecture and offers much better scalability than traditional MPP architecture. In practice, this architecture will likely outperform other architectures for clusters that have more than 100 or 200 nodes.

Critical Open Source Technologies Used by Uber

Uber began adopting Hadoop in 2015, later than most companies for the simple reason that Uber is younger. Our "youth" turned out to be a unique advantage, helping us to avoid pitfalls along the paths taken by older companies and enabling us to combine our work in Hadoop with newer technologies like Spark. The resulting combination of Hadoop and Spark give Uber the reliability and performance we need as the company continues to scale across the world.

Although Map-Reduce solved the scalability problem, it is a lower-level API than what most data customers need. To provide a higher-level abstraction—SQL language—to Uber's internal teams, we adopted Hive, the most widely used SQL on Hadoop solution.

Although Hive is pretty scalable and reliable, it is not fast enough for interactive queries. In 2016, Uber adopted Presto for interactive SQL queries. Although Hive is more scalable, Presto runs much faster. Presto queries can finish in seconds, if not tenths of seconds, compared with Hive jobs, which can run for minutes or hours.

In 2017, to take advantage of both Hive's reliability and maturity and Spark's speed and ease-of-use, we are seriously considering moving from Hive to Hive on Spark, a combination of the two. Hive on Spark provides the Hive interface with Spark as the underlying engine.

In addition to the aforementioned batch-oriented systems, Uber also has a streaming analytical stack powered by Kafka and Samza, which are open source projects with origins in LinkedIn. Kafka is used as a message bus and Samza is used as the basis for a streaming processing engine. Uber started with Kafka version 0.7 and later migrated to 0.8 for better reliability and scale. We also made several important improvements to the Kafka replication layer called MirrorMaker (*https://github.com/uber/uReplicator*). Uber is probably one of the largest users of Kafka in the world right now.

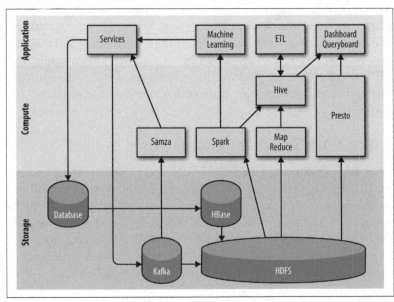

Figure 10-1. A subset of Uber's data stack

Making Data Democratic

Now, let us take a look at how Uber's data systems helped the company achieve data democracy. Data democracy means that various teams can utilize data for innovation regardless of their level of technical skill. How you make data democratic depends on the composition of employees. What percentage of data users are technical versus nontechnical? Is it 80 percent technical and 20 percent nontechnical? Or the other way around? The ratio of technical to nontechnical users will determine your data democratization strategy.

When it comes to handling data, technical users often prefer self-serve platforms, which are easier to customize, whereas nontechnical users generally prefer manual hand-holding from the data team via accessible processes and support. At Uber, we have employees in both categories using our data stack to build and refine our services. As a result, we had to offer both options.

Self-Serve Platforms

There are many ways to serve data on a web browser. Dashboards are very popular among nontechnical users; however, dashboards—even the interactive ones—are limited in functionality. To combat these limitations at Uber, we built a browser-based SQL access tool.

It's very important to enforce sound controls on a self-serve platform. Ensuring compliance, privacy, and security is the most obvious reason, but scalability and efficiency are also a strong consideration. The data cluster might not have enough capacity to give everyone the computational resources they require, especially when a company is scaling rapidly.

Supporting Users

A self-serve platform is the first component of data democratization; the second is implementing good processes and support systems. For Uber's use case, we decided the appropriate combination to meet these needs was a specialized, full-time data ops team, as well as dedicated time from rest of the data team.

This combination is important. The data ops team builds very strong relationships with users. It understands users' business use cases as well as their pain points with the self-serve platform. Responsibilities include building and improving communication channels with users and sending out periodical announcements on changes to the platform.

Time commitment from the rest of the data team is also important because it is responsible for tackling more difficult technical problems that can severely affect processes. In particular, senior members on the data team have deep dive sessions with key users to ensure that the end-to-end solution and long-term architecture are sufficient to meet users' needs. These sessions and the team's close attention to detail gives the rest of the data team direct visibility into user needs and experiences, helping to shape the long-term direction of the product.

Although Uber has made great progress in data democratization, our journey is just getting started. Check out the Uber Engineering Blog (*https://eng.uber.com/*) to stay informed of project updates.

CHAPTER 11

Twitter: When Everything Happens in Real Time

Karthik Ramasamy, cofounder of Streamlio,
former engineering manager for real-time
compute at Twitter

Twitter is all about real time. So, it needs infrastructure to handle data in real time, to do analytics, and provide insights in real time. As engineering manager for real-time compute at Twitter, I managed the infrastructures that facilitate the real-time analytics computation. My team managed all of the infrastructure and the tools needed to do this.

I came to Twitter in 2013 when Twitter acquired my company, which was doing real-time processing of GPS, or spatial, data. So, when Twitter wanted to have technology for processing real-time data, it acquired us, and we came to build its next-generation real-time platform.

Twitter Develops Heron

Called Heron (*https://github.com/twitter/heron*), our real-time, distributed, and fault-tolerant stream-processing engine has powered all of Twitter's real-time analytics since 2014. After it was deployed, incident reports dropped by an order of magnitude, demonstrating that Heron was both reliable and scalable. Because Heron is API-compatible with the popular Apache Storm, no code changes are required to migrate to Heron. Twitter open-sourced Heron in mid-2016.

When my team joined Twitter, the need for real-time analytics was growing exponentially. The company had one of the first implementations of the real-time processing system called Apache Storm, another popular software project that was open sourced by Twitter in 2011.

But Storm had three primary shortcomings: it was person-to-hours intensive to support, organizations couldn't reliably run it in a monitored cluster at scale, and it couldn't handle diverse use cases.

We would receive pages almost every night in the wee hours because it was so unreliable. And precisely because it was so unreliable, my team would devote significant resources to a single job, even though that job might not warrant that much attention. Thus, the cost of running individual jobs was high.

Ironically, the more resources that were dedicated to a job, the more unreliable that job became. Such was the status of the situation there when we started. After looking at the various options, I decided that writing new software from scratch would give Twitter more independent control and ownership than trying to adapt existing open source software. So, we decided to write our own software, which we did pretty quickly—within just nine months.

After we moved Heron into production, my team was able to reduce the number of incidents tenfold. In fact, within the two and half years Heron was in production, my team experienced only four or five incidents in total. In short, Heron had proven to be completely reliable.

By having a stable system like Heron to analyze all of our data, the data-driven nature of Twitter's operations gave us continuous visibility across all our operations. Twitter is therefore a stronger company because its team is able to make decisions based on data rather than "gut feel."

For example, we used data coming from logs to analyze failures across datacenters. If one datacenter failed for any reason, we analyzed that data to figure out when the failure occurred, and to immediately cut traffic over to the other datacenter. This type of instant failover improved the overall availability of Twitter.

Heron is all about processing data in motion. In other words, Twitter's data is continuously streaming. They do all the outtakes and all the cancellations on the data in real time, because there are multiple different analytics that people do on data. With these *streaming analytics*, as soon as the data is produced, the analytics are performed on the spot, actually as the data is moving.

But Twitter also had a need for *interactive analytics*, where Twitter stores the data. Users can query it and get results quickly enough so that they can do ad hoc exploration of the data.

And then there was also a need for *batch analytics*, which refers to analytics of the more traditional kind, in which a particular job is run for several hours or several days until the results are available.

Although Heron took care of streaming analytics, Twitter didn't have "great" solutions in place for interactive or batch analytics when I joined the company. So, after closing out the Heron development, my team initiated another project so people would quickly query data at rest at a large scale.

We were using a commercial solution that was not cutting edge enough for all the requirements that we had, because of the sheer size of the data that we routinely handle. Finally, we chose Presto to deliver interactive ad hoc exploration on top of the data stored at rest. It took a year, but it's now running in production.

Presto is used as an ad hoc exploration-for-quality tool by different teams, especially by data scientists, who are constantly analyzing the data. How did the ads perform yesterday versus today? Is there any correlation between the placements of the ads versus when the ads are shown? Twitter is continuously exploring that data to figure out interesting relationships.

Presto is also used to enhance product features, by trying to identify where the problems in a product might lie, so that data-driven decisions can be made when deciding on future product direction.

Seven Different Use Cases for Real-Time Streaming Analytics

Heron enabled seven use cases for the real-time analytics:

Real-time ETL

While the data is moving, Twitter can extract it, transform it, and analyze it in real time.

Real-time continuous business intelligence

As the data is continually coming in, Twitter can use that data to identify where specifically the Tweets are coming from, and break it down by what type of operating system the user is on, whether it's PC or mobile, Android, or iPhone. Twitter can also use this type of analysis to learn how the ads are performing—this is very important because our monetization comes by way of ads. So, all ads are compared in real time.

Product abuse

Twitter is constantly analyzing Twitter data to find fake or abusive accounts, so we can take proactive action and expose those accounts as well as the tweets.

Real-time trending

Twitter also continuously computes trends that are emerging out of Twitter by examining all the Tweet data. Breaking news and all the hashtag trends are continuously computed and bubbled up to serve in the Twitter app itself.

Real-time machine learning

In this use case, Twitter does real-time predictive modeling. The model is continuously updated as data comes in, via ads, for example.

Media

Twitter manages a lot of photos and videos, and features are extracted from them in real time and used to classify media based on the features that they have.

Operations

Because Twitter has hundreds and thousands of machines, we use the data coming from those missions to analyze and predict whether there is an impending failure based on the data being received about the drives. We review memory as well as the network on all the videos, too.

Advice to Companies Seeking to Be Data-Driven

You can collect everything today, but if you don't manage it carefully, it can quickly get out of hand. You need a dedicated team that decides what data needs to be collected, and how to organize and expose it.

Data-driven decisions are going to be the foundation of business actions across the board in the near future. Not only from cost savings and operational efficiencies points of view, but also from a product point of view.

Which products are working? Which are not working? How well is a particular team performing? All aspects of building a product are going to be measured by data.

But to do this, organizations need a formal process or formal data team that is centralized. And someone must be in charge of data collection and management—which is probably one of the most difficult things to do. The economics of collecting and storing data are such that you can collect everything today, but if you don't manage it carefully, it can quickly get out of hand. You need a dedicated team that decides what data needs to be collected, and how to organize and expose it.

Another team should focus on ETL. This team transforms data into something palatable for users to consume. And of course, you need tools to do that. Whether you want a data-addressed interactive exploration, or you want to do batch analytics or streaming analytics, each type of analysis will have a different team and corresponding infrastructure, the latter of which is managed by the infrastructure team.

Finally, you expose all these easy-to-use interfaces to data professionals like data scientists, who are the ones analyzing the data so that they can convert it into actionable insights. Then you'd get the appropriate actionable insights to the appropriate teams—whether a product team, or something else. In many cases, data scientists could be embedded into these teams. The data scientist, in turn, uses all the infrastructure tools and the data provided by the data acquisition and infrastructure teams.

Looking Ahead

Today, I am considering a number of new ideas, especially in terms of detecting anomalies in data. For example, instead of saying, "I'm looking for an anomaly," we want to automatically find anomalies when they occur, and make them visible so that we can do a forward-looking analysis of why something happened.

Anomalies have occurred within several contexts, especially during streaming. One of Twitter's major headaches is when a server is not running optimally. A job starts backing up, or it begins to lag, and that causes issues from a reliability standpoint. One of my goals was to build a system in which Twitter can identify problems *as they are occurring*, automatically realize a bad host is causing issues, and select a good host to run. Thus, the job will begin running faster without us having to do any manual intervention. Although some companies have attempted to detect anomalies in batch mode, in real-time it's a big task.

A second initiative that I considered was to implement "self-healing" in a streaming infrastructure, in which jobs can heal themselves and continuously provide analytics without any manual intervention. So, how can a job identify problems itself, and correct itself? These were, and are, exciting initiatives.

CHAPTER 12

Capture All Data, Decide What to Do with It Later: My Experience at eBay

by Debashis Saha, former vice president of commerce platform infrastructure at eBay

NOTE Debashis Saha is a former employee of eBay. The views expressed here are his own.

What *can't* you buy on eBay? You name it, you can find it on the global online marketplace. Four nights in a luxury condo in Telluride? Credit for Uber rides? A Winnebago motor home? Or perhaps clothes, kitchen gadgets, computers, and just about anything else you can think of for personal or business use.

All the activities of all the millions of buyers and sellers—165 million active users at the end of 2016[1] to be exact, with more than 1 billion simultaneous listings[2]—are captured as part of eBay's standard operating procedures: capture all data and decide whether—and how—to use it later.

---

1 *https://www.statista.com/statistics/242235/number-of-ebays-total-active-users/*

2 *http://expandedramblings.com/index.php/ebay-stats/*

When I joined eBay 10 years ago, I was glad to see that a data-driven culture was already ingrained in the organization. In particular, I was delighted to see that eBay already had executive support for centralizing data. It made my role to build, manage, and operate everything to do with data for eBay—from datacenters to frameworks, to data infrastructure, networks, and all data services—much easier.

At eBay, we produce three fundamental types of data. First is the transactional data: every time a user buys, bids, or otherwise takes action on the site, data is generated and collected. Transactional data produces tens of millions of data points every day.

The second kind of data is behavioral data: the ways our users interact with eBay. A lot of behavioral actions—browsing, clicking on a link in an email, or monitoring a particular auction—eventually lead to the transaction, but at eBay, we consider that a different kind of data. The behavioral data, which is both semi-structured and unstructured, is orders of magnitude larger in volume than the transactional data.

The third kind of data is system data: this is data that represents the way our systems operate and interact with each other, which includes but is not limited to their health (security, performance, availability, diagnostics) and more, in order to produce a characterization of the systems and humans working together to deliver eBay's customer experiences.

Before I joined the company, eBay was primarily a transaction data–driven company. All the transaction data was put in one central data warehouse that was managed by a centralized team, and all decisions and reporting came out of that team. For example, the warehouse tracked such things as how many Pez dispensers were sold during a given period, the average selling price, and other parameters of transactions.

Back then, the transactional data warehouse was very small. Still, I feel that having a centralized data warehouse and supporting team was a critical early decision—and a great one. The only issue was the velocity of change to data models. Whenever we had logic changes within the site, it took us longer to make changes in the reports than we would have liked.

At that point, we were not storing any of our user behavior data. Instead, we were throwing it out. This was in late 2007, and Hadoop was just coming into the picture within the industry but had not yet matured to the point where it was mainstream.

So, when I arrived, the question was how could we use all the behavioral data in a way that could drive personalization—which would in turn drive better customer engagement and delight customers? The drive to do more with data came from the top of the company. eBay's CFO was particularly interested in how to use data to understand how the business could be improved.

You need three elements to build a data-driven company: extremely strong executive support; centralized reporting of business data; and high-quality data.

About the first and second points: if directives to use centralized data are not coming from the top down, you're going to get different answers for the same questions, and people are going to begin questioning the data itself. Then, of course, there's the question "is the data *right*?" The quality of data is extremely important so that people trust it. Data governance plays a huge part in building a data-driven company.

Ensuring "CAP-R" in Your Data Infrastructure

Although we did a fairly good job of centralizing the data, we soon realized that wasn't enough. We also had to create a centralized data *infrastructure* and a team to manage it. The data infrastructure team provided the data platforms like databases and connectivity from the online to offline data storage and processing systems. The most important aspect, however, was providing system capacity for the data team, and centralizing the budgets for data growth. This way, not only the data team but also the data infrastructure and platform teams ensured that we always have proper capacity, proper performance, availability, and reliability for our data systems.

Most companies will—like eBay—go through humongous data growth. If you are not able to keep up with the infrastructure needs and the public clouds or private cloud capacity you need, as well as the budget to grow that capacity, you're going to end up with a siloed data infrastructure. And that will make your ability to come up with consistent and smart decisions impossible.

I call this capability "CAP-R": capacity, availability, performance, and reliability. We had a lot of growing pains in this, but with a data-driven culture, I think people forgive you for the sins that you go through when you grow. Is there enough capacity? Is performance adequate? Is the system running properly? All of these questions need to be answered with "yes" or analysts will be unhappy.

What should companies do that are just beginning their data-driven journeys? Embrace the fact that it's going to be rocky. The data will never be perfect. But if you have invested in data quality, and data engineers to ensure you always have a reconciliation process to fight drift, the credibility of your data will increase over time and provide ever-expanding value.

Organizational Structure

When I was at eBay, the analytics team reported up through the CFO. We organized our data analysts around the business units— the groups that support our various business products.

When companies are small, centralization supports their ability to build momentum. It also creates a consumer relationship between the providers and the users of data. Somebody's clamoring for the data and then somebody produces the data to meet that need, and that's a good thing. But it begins to break down when you have product managers and other employees who want direct access to the data. The centralized team can't service them all fast enough.

Then you enter a phase in which self-service data access becomes important. Every company is going to struggle with that eventually. Who is the end user for the data? Who gets to be on the user side of self-service?

In other words, does your data exist to simply make your data analysts more productive, or are you concerned about giving access to data to product managers, development managers, and everyone else in the organization?

I championed the fact that data is there for everybody. Of course, eBay has specialized people—the employees we called data analysts —who are experts in the use of the data. However, more and more, we realized that the regular questions about products, product help, product metrics, and all the other things that are routinely asked should be done by product managers and other employees.

In such cases, a simple SQL-like interface, or simple out-of-the-box reports and graphical representations of data that can be achieved with today's visualization tools provide more self-service ways of slicing and dicing data.

But now the challenge is that your data needs and data infrastructure needs really become extremely high. This was where having a strong relationship with the CFO was very important. As it turned out, the cost of capturing, storing, and making data available was always one of our bigger budget line items.

Governing and Democratizing Data

We had a very open culture of publishing our data architecture and inviting discussion about it, given the hundreds of data tools available.

The next step we took was to optimize the customer journey by utilizing the behavioral data we already had been routinely storing but not using: How could eBay use experimentation and behavioral data to create customer segments and improve the customer experience?

This is where analysts can't support the data-driven journey because this is more of a question for product managers with deep domain expertise.

To facilitate this, we took a survey of the tools we'd been using, to identify which ones would be most helpful when "democratizing" data beyond the centralized data team. We had a very open culture of publishing our data architecture and inviting discussion about it, given the hundreds of data tools available. We asked our users, "Which one do you use? Which one you don't use?" It was very important to us that the dialogue never died. A hallmark of a good data-driven culture is an openness to discussion, and to constantly ask, "How can we do better?"

This is where you begin to ask "what is democratizing"? Are you democratizing data? Are you democratizing services that act on the data? You need to be clear about that.

My viewpoint is that you need to prioritize democratizing data over services. However, I believe that data governance comes first. You should be able to ask, "In this one hour, how many clicks happened? How many experiments happened? What are the ROI events that are happening?" All of those need to be carefully curated with good governance, and then democratized in so-called "golden data."

This golden data is the data that the centralized data team has certi-fied as being high-quality, accurate, and current. There are three types of golden data: online golden data, golden data in motion, and golden data at rest. The lineage across the three needs to be carefully governed and published so that anybody in the company can use the three types of data to create reports. Then, golden data can be used to create services that are shared across teams.

Think of the data itself first and then the data services, and you get almost an illusion of infinite capacity for employees to access and use the data.

Additionally, you need to bring data services back to the data source so that others can use them. Otherwise, you'll begin seeing teams developing very interesting data that cannot be reused. The reusabil-ity of data—not only through services but the data itself—becomes an important function of the data governance.

Personalization: A Key Benefit of Data-Driven Culture

Making all the data available to everyone helped eBay accelerate its journey to use real-time data across every product. This is where the behavioral data came in.

If you go to the home page personalizations of individual users, you can see the individual recommendations that eBay performs: what products to look for, to consider bidding on, and to buy. eBay also uses the behavioral data to drive customer engagement via its Cus-tomer Relationship Management (CRM) system, by determining which emails and notifications are sent to different users. The democratization of data made all these capabilities extremely easy to create. For example, eBay Deals is an extremely big part of eBay, where sellers can promote items from their stores that are available at discounted prices for 24 hours. To ensure that eBay Deals are as lucrative as possible for sellers, eBay uses behavioral data to pinpoint which buyers are likely to be the most interested in a particular deal.

eBay is unique in that it enables anybody to conduct business and supports both sellers and buyers with its vast volumes of both trans-actional and behavioral data. We believe in democratization of the commerce experience, whereby everybody can have equal opportu-nity in the market. If you believe in that, you must open up your data and create a group platform where sellers and others can use data to extend their experiences. eBay is continuing on its journey to open up even more of its data to users.

Building Data Tools and Giving Back to the Open Source Community

As previously mentioned, eBay's journey to becoming a data-driven company was first based on transactional data, which came in the form of daily reports to interested stakeholders. At that point, if you're only exposing the reports and building APIs on the reports, you're interfacing with the data at the wrong level. However, if you open up that data, you can optimize access to it. This is where visualization tools become important.

Many of the commercialized data tools in the market were simply not sufficient to what we needed to fully open up its data for democratization. So, a huge part of what we did was drive development of open source tools, and contribute them to the community.

So, we built Apache Kylin (*http://kylin.apache.org/*) and Apache Eagle (*https://eagle.apache.org/*) and contributed both to the Apache Open Source Foundation. These have graduated to be Apache Top level projects.

We had a classic Online Analytic Processing (OLAP) use case that we were doing over and over again, and traditional databases were just not good enough to serve our data volumes. We created Kylin to provide subsecond results on queries involving lots of data—terabytes of data, in some cases.

Eagle was developed as a system to process the logs and metrics from all operational big data systems (and later generalized for any data system) in real time. It can be used for real-time analysis and alerting in a broad set of problems ranging from system health, performance to security.

We also developed and open sourced Pulsar (*http://gopulsar.io/*), which is a technology used for real-time analytic processing. That, combined with the ecosystem of all the other Hadoop products (Druid, Elastic Search, and others), grew our reputation in the industry for having an open-source culture. We would have debates about which tools to add to the data architecture. Then, we focused on how everybody could be productive on these tools.

However, we were very careful to avoid creating multiple frameworks that did the same thing. We focused on having the platform team provide a very simple, easy-to-use library and easy-to-use end points, focusing heavily on productivity in two forms. One was data productivity for data engineers, and the second was developer productivity because developers also want to use the same data to enhance the experiences that they are creating in the products.

The Importance of Machine Learning

Data is our most critical asset. You hear our CFO and CEO say this over and over again in leadership meetings. Having said that, how do we take advantage of it? It's important that a data-driven culture is not just about reporting: it's about using data in a programmatic fashion. More and more, you are beginning to see how you can use data to train models. That's where machine learning comes into play. Without it, you cannot unlock the potential of data.

Two things happened to make machine learning possible. First, improved data infrastructures like Hadoop and the cloud made it possible to train on years of data in a very short timeframe. This led to deep learning through complex machine-learning algorithms. Take speech recognition, which has improved over recent years from 95 percent accuracy to 99 percent accuracy. Those four percentage points made it extremely trustworthy for people to accept the results of the machine learning.

Second, companies began thinking of machine learning infrastructures as extensions to their data infrastructures. There are machine learning experts at eBay, but what we want to do is centralize the platforms for machine learning and have them be part of the data infrastructure team itself. This means eBay must cross-pollinate machine learning expertise with data-processing capabilities. If it were a job requirement, data scientists, data infrastructure, backend engineers—all of these are beginning to blend. You need a group of people, expert in all of these things to be able to push a data-driven culture in a company.

Looking Ahead

Today, eBay's plan is to integrate machine learning into each and every piece of data in the eBay product infrastructure, and to understand how to create a more complex and more intelligent form of data processing. The company is now working on building infrastructure that it can use to promote self-service machine learning, reusable machine learning, and extensible machine learning. That's the next frontier that eBay is trying to get to for analysts, product managers, business people, and developers.

A Podcast Interview Transcript

This is a transcript of a conversation between Qubole cofounder and CEO, Ashish Thusoo, and O'Reilly's Jon Bruner.

Jon: *I'm here today with Ashish Thusoo. He's the cofounder and CEO of Qubole. Welcome on.*

Ashish: Thanks, Jon.

Jon: *We're talking today about building a data-driven culture, which is something that you've done at Facebook and it's something that you think a lot about now at Qubole. Could you tell us a bit about what it is to have data-driven culture?*

Ashish: Yeah, sure. In my point of view, data-driven culture is a combination of processes, people, and technology that allows companies to bring data in their day-to-day conversation. Traditionally, when data was not available, a lot of decision-making in companies, both at the technical level, as well as the strategic level, would happen through gut feeling, through intuition, where there will be some expert in the room saying that, "I understand this landscape and this is what we should do." I think over a period of time, what has become clear that along with intuition, you need to augment that with testing those intuitions and those hypotheses with data. That is what a data-driven culture enables.

Companies that augment that intuition and gut feeling along with testing through data and then using data to arrive at certain decisions whether for tactical purposes or strategic purposes, those companies that create that type of culture essentially become data-driven companies. It's been proven again and again and there's a lot of literature around this, which shows that companies that embrace that type of an approach ultimately become much more profitable from different metrics of success. They become much more successful as compared to companies who are just relying on intuition or gut feel or certain expert opinions inside the company itself, so that is what I mean by data-driven culture. It is essentially a confluence of a positive confluence of people, processes, and technologies that puts data into the conversations that companies have whether they're for strategic decision-making or tactical reasons.

Jon: *It's a matter of avoiding, in part, what is sometimes called HIPPO —the "highest paid person's opinion."*

Ashish: That is correct, correct. The HIPPOs are very dangerous and data essentially makes the conversation much more objective as opposed to subjective.

Jon: *Excellent.*

Ashish: Sort of [inaudible 00:02:09] and it empowers people to actually talk about issues in such a standard way, as opposed to in a subjective way.

Jon: *It's kind of a mindset that can spread throughout a whole company and become a way that any employee contributes by looking at the data and making, as you say, more objective decisions rather than perhaps embedding themselves unproductively in a hierarchy or feeling like they can't contribute.*

Ashish: That is correct. It does empower employees and very importantly, it also...What it does is that when you are in a room making a decision or talking about a certain issue, then the natural question...Whenever there's such a discussion, there are a lot of questions that arise and the natural recourse to that should be, "Hey, let's look at the data and figure out whether some of these assumptions are correct," or "If we do such and such thing, what will be the effect? What does the data show us?" That type of realization across the company, across different levels of the company, across different functions of the company, once that type of realization sips in, that's what creates a data-driven culture.

Jon: *Obviously, you need more than just the culture, right? You need sort of the infrastructure in place and the tools that make this possible which for most people, "I have been thinking about this." They realize that isn't so much an easy thing to do, right?*

Ashish: That's correct. Like I said, it's a confluence of a bunch of things. It's a confluence of people, processes, and technology. There is definitely need for tools and infrastructure to support this type of an environment because if the infrastructure support is not there or tool support is not there and people cannot get to data, then the easiest course is to say, "Okay, we don't have enough data. Let's make an assumption and move forward." To me, a data delayed is data denied. It works like that. Also, making sure that data is available and infrastructure is available for people to use our data, to test that hypothesis, to ask the questions of that data, and come up with answers. Making that self-service on a broad scale is very, very important and very central to this transformation, and then, of course, it's not just that. There is transformation that is needed on the people and processes side as well, but without the technology, you cannot achieve it.

Jon: *For the listeners who are maybe thinking about building a data-driven culture and plotting out their strategy for what they need, what are the essential technological pieces that you need?*

Ashish: This is a great question. If you look at past companies, a lot of data infrastructure that supports this type of an environment was always gated. You would have companies a certain amount of data and structure in place and then a team sitting within the infrastructure and the users and this team would be the gatekeeper of this infrastructure. The reasons for that were various...There were various different reasons. There were reasons around infrastructure could not scale, so the team was always a little apprehensive of just opening it up to everyone because it would be brought down by a certain query or certain things like that. There were maybe not enough tooling for them to audit and figure out who's using this infrastructure and what way or the [inaudible 00:05:15] infrastructure and so on and so forth.

There were various different reasons, but in order to really get a truly data-driven culture and be successful around it, you need to invert the problem. You need to have the infrastructure be self-service to the users and the team should be supporting the infrastructure. The data team should be supporting the infrastructure by sitting behind the infrastructure and be responsible for making sure that this infrastructure is available to everyone. There are enough [toolings 00:05:38] and tool infrastructure or tool integrations done with this infrastructure so it can be used by different data personnel, as whether they're an engineer or data scientist or an analyst or maybe a line of business user, who is trying to interact with this infrastructure, there's enough of tooling and tool integration available there. There's enough governance and policy and access control in place so that they can, for sensitive datasets, they can silo that off and stuff like that.

All of that should be put together by the data team into the infrastructure and they should sit behind the infrastructure and support it and make the infrastructure self-service. That is the most fundamental thing that is needed in order to take the first baby step towards getting to data-driven culture. I saw that firsthand at Facebook. Facebook had ... When we started in Facebook, this is back in 2007, the infrastructure was very much like most companies handle that data infrastructure today. Essentially, [inaudible 00:06:34] data teams setting between the users and the infrastructure on the other end. Facebook was an exponentially growing company and for them, for that environment, that configuration became a bottleneck.

We had to chase the configuration. We brought in [inaudible 00:06:50]. We created Hive. We created a whole bunch of other [inaudible 00:06:53] to make sure that we got out from setting between the users and the infrastructure. We made the infrastructure self-service and then we were supporting the infrastructure from behind and that had a big role in making it data-driven. I think the same sort of a transformation is possible for every other company who wants to become data-driven today. The first step really is to think about self-service data infrastructure.

Jon: *For the self-service culture that you would be looking to build, where employees are empowered to go in and look at the data and make decisions based on it, that suggest that perhaps you also need a different kind of employee or maybe some training for employees or a different mindset for the employees when you compare it to perhaps to a more traditional mechanism, where you have like a business intelligence department and you're just sending them queries. How do you wind up with the right people for that?*

Ashish: You're absolutely right. This is both training problem as well as expectation setting. Training as well as a process problem, I would say. Every employee wants to get to their answers quickly. That is a big [inaudible 00:07:58] to dangle in front of the employee saying that if you embrace this type of transformation where you have a tooling in place or infrastructure in place where you can go and access this data and try to answer some of these questions. If you embrace this type of a culture, you will get to your answers much more quickly and your productivity will increase. You'd be able to do your job faster as opposed to running to a central team.

That is very critical but then all these employees come in different forms of expertise. Some of them maybe very comfortable thinking about data if you're a data engineer or a data analyst or a data scientist. Data is your life and you can think about data left and right and you can do hypothesis testing run, queries, and transformation and stuff like that. For them, this transformation becomes very easy and all that they need is a mechanism for an infrastructure where they can go in and not just be able to query the data but also data discovery, how they're able to figure out what datasets to use, and so on and so forth. That is what they need.

Now, there are certain other set of employees who may not be data-driven and who typically interact with...They have very fixed queries and, essentially, they are trained in the parameters of the queries and they're not asking different types of questions, but they are parameterizing those questions in a different way.

Jon: *Sure. They're taking a question that maybe their manager or someone else in the organization has created and they're just sort of rerunning it in a different form.*

Ashish: Supposed there's an employee he wants to look at...In a web company, for example, they want to look at monthly activities or something like that.

Jon: *Sure.*

Ashish: It's the same question but for different months, [inaudible 00:09:36] different answers and things like that. I think for those employees, you can put together on this infrastructure, you can create applets, farms, there are a lot of [dashboarding 00:09:47] tools and reporting tools that you can use to drive that type of thing, but then you have to make those assets self-service. You don't have to hide those assets behind the data team but you have to maybe give them an interface where they can enter some of these parameters and the infrastructure is able to deliver that question, whether that is through a dynamic report or whether that is through a simple data form or something like that, you can do that and we did do that at Facebook also to some degree.

You can address some of those things where the interface is matched to the capabilities of the employee, but all of these interfaces should be self-serviced. That is very critical. Once you train your employees around those interfaces, it's easy to train people with interfaces that are in tuned with their capabilities. The motivation you're able to show them is those interfaces, they can get to their answers much more quickly. What used to take them weeks now can take them few minutes or hours to attain and I think that in Facebook, and we have seen this in Qubole also with a lot of our customers, once you put those tools in place in front of these employees and show them the benefits in terms of how it increases the agility, the effects are transformational and everybody embraces it. Nobody fights it.

Jon: *The key is, first, to sort of present the value proposition to the employees and show them why this is very valuable.*

Ashish: Right.

Jon: *You've talked about Qubole and what you're doing with this data and intelligence infrastructure as the third wave in cloud computing. I wonder if you could talk about what that means.*

Ashish: We are living in a day and age where there's a lot of disruption happening in terms of how companies consume applications and infrastructure. We started off with mainframe computing, then mainframe computing moved towards client-server computing and that is all the basis of datacenters and now, we are in this age of data, of cloud computing. The cloud computing transformation itself has been going on for a long time, but it has happened fundamentally in three waves.

The first wave, which is successful and which is the pioneers of cloud computing, were companies like Salesforce.com which are applications. These are SaaS applications. They were catered towards solving a certain business problem, and in the case of Salesforce, it does a CRM application catered towards a business user and as a full solution that was hosted in the cloud, in the Salesforce cloud, and essentially, it became a SaaS solution and sow the seeds of what has now become full-blown cloud computing.

After that, the second wave was started much more bottoms-up which has been pioneered by AWS, and essentially, that has been, "Hey, we did application and service, CRM service. You know what? Let's try to do IT as a service. Can we do compute and storage and those types of things," or tools, load balances, and stuff like that as a service. All the building blocks that are needed to create applications, that is the second wave of cloud computing and that is really a big disruption to IT and that is what we call as infrastructure as a service wave. I think that wave is playing out and is aggressively disrupting the datacenter world.

Now, on top of this wave, since...What did the second wave achieve? It essentially converted hardware and infrastructure into APIs, so into software. As a result, things became much more on-demand, much more agile, much more flexible, and so on and so forth, but since hardware and infrastructure got converted into software, there was an opportunity for companies like us to leverage that and automate complex pieces of infrastructure. In our case, it was data infrastructure, so [inaudible 00:13:24] looking at the emergence of cloud phones built on full-blown data platforms like us. Data platforms is just an example. There could be other platforms as well, which are built on top of this infrastructure, which are utilizing the API...The infrastructure as a software paradigm to automate a lot of the complexity out from this infrastructure and creating platforms, which then users can now use to build their applications, to build their hypothesis and things like that.

I think that is the third wave, which has now started to become more and more useful. There are companies like us who are essentially doing that. A lot of cloud vendors are creating machine learning as a service that is catering towards people who are trying to put together machine learning for creating letter applications. You are starting to see a reemergence of platform as a service to some degree, and that I think is the third wave of cloud computing, and that has been possible because infrastructure as a service has become so successful and has also trained people to think in a different way, or rather has provided an alternative for people to think in a different way as when they think the word, infrastructure. Think of it more from an angle of an API as opposed to thinking of that as machines and hardware and so on and so forth.

Jon: *Right, so because the infrastructure itself has moved into the cloud, it's now become possible to take these applications, the software that depended on being very close to the infrastructure, and move it to the cloud as well, is that right?*

Ashish: That is correct. The software is moving to the cloud. What is also fundamental is that these infrastructures, cloud infrastructure, is so different from datacenters or datacenter infrastructure simply because the cloud is all about APIs being the frontend of the infrastructure as opposed to machine and stuff like that. Now, the next generation of software and platforms that are being built on top of this infrastructure, looks fundamentally very different and the things that they can do are fundamentally very different from what was possible in the previous era. A case, for example, is Qubole, right? We have been talking about automation of our cloud service. Other infrastructure comes on-demand. It responds to what the user says, and then we spin up infrastructure on-demand, and so on and so forth, which did not happen in the previous era because the previous era was more about, "Let me pull infrastructure in place first and then flip my applications through it."

Now, with the second wave of cloud computing which is infrastructure service, we are now able to build the third wave, where applications are able to clear the infrastructure on the fly to fill the application, as opposed to the other way around.

Jon: *Interesting. You've mentioned Facebook a few times here. You and your cofounder built the original analytics infrastructure at Facebook back around 2007. I wonder if you could talk a little about what that entailed and how that changed the culture inside Facebook after you implemented it.*

Ashish: Sure. Both me and Michael founded [inaudible 00:16:19]. We were at Facebook from 2007 to 2011 and [inaudible 00:16:25], we essentially built out the...We started off with this premise, start creating a data infrastructure which was not self-service or be detrimental in the growth of the company itself, and we wanted to create something much more self-service, and that is what we built it out there.

Jon: *As you pointed out earlier, Facebook, at that time, was just growing incredibly fast. You couldn't possibly-*

Ashish: Incredibly fast. That infrastructure, to give you the impact that infrastructure had, when we left, 30 percent of the company would use that infrastructure on monthly basis to answer questions. These were thousands of users. It's a 5,000-people company. That infrastructure has further grown now and still supports a similar percentage of the company heavily and in terms of how they use data and stuff like that. Their transformation was very, very...It was very start. When we started, I still remember before we build this out, data was a big problem. Facebook did not have a problem of being a data culture company. All the people wanted to use data in some way or a form, but since there was no self-service infrastructure, they were very, very restrained on what data they would get. As a result, decisions will be taken very intuitively. [inaudible 00:17:47] launched this particular feature, see what happens.

Jon: *Right, right.*

Ashish: With that infrastructure now, all the decision-making has become much more data-driven. Not just decision-making, that infrastructure had a profound impact on a lot of strategic initiatives within the company, whether it was growing the network, growing the Facebook user base, a lot of things, lot of hypothesis testing used to happen that infrastructure, how to model users, who to reach out to, what [inaudible 00:18:13] to reach out to, and so on and so forth. For monetization and ad targeting, what ads to show to which users, and so on and so forth. That happened on that infrastructure. Recommendations around which people you should friend depending upon your friend, a lot of that was some of the models were built there, [inaudible 00:18:31] were built there.

The [inaudible 00:18:33] what happened is that once you made that infrastructure self-service, it started to penetrate into various different efforts in Facebook whether they're product efforts or strategic efforts and that is basically what happens with self-service. Then it became truly data-driven. There was a time then...We moved from not using to a time where people would just turn queries this infrastructure to figure out the answers in real time and then make decisions.

Jon: *Right.*

Ashish: It's very, very transformational outcome.

Jon: *Yeah. You can look even at Facebook's product and see how data-driven the products themselves are. You can imagine that having such a data-driven culture inside the company is expressed in some sense in the sophistication of the data-motivated products.*

Ashish: That's right. That's right. Again, what I should have said before, there was never any doubt about using data in Facebook. It was just a matter of making this data available and putting together self-service infrastructure that really [inaudible 00:19:32] that data [inaudible 00:19:32].

Jon: *Right.*

Ashish: The effects were profound.

Jon: *Right, right. I imagine that a lot of early stage companies like Facebook was around 2007, you had tons and tons of data but it was sort of accessible only to handful of users who are perhaps hitting the data directly to make queries and then answering questions that came in from other people. Is that the bottleneck that you referred to?*

Ashish: Yes. Because the infrastructure was built like that, because it was not self-service, because they were not easy to use interfaces, because it was not super scalable at the backend, so if you open it up to everyone, the infrastructure will fall off flat on its face, because of all those reasons, there was a small set of users sitting between the infrastructure and the other users and all the other users had to constantly go back to This...This, you call this the data team and the data team will give them the data. Clearly, that is unsustainable.

Data team will become the bottleneck and many users will not get to their data fast enough and so the recourse was to look at some sample or datasets here or there or make some good intuitive decisions and many times, the [inaudible 00:20:38] did not go out to be right, but with data entering and when data became so accessible, not only did that decision-making become more accurate, it also became more rapid because now you could...Without being...You could fail fast. You didn't have to really get your thing right completely but you could [inaudible 00:21:02], change your strategy and stuff like that.

Jon: *Right, right. Imagine that since you are building tools that promote sort of a data-driven culture, that you must think a great deal about producing a data-driven culture inside Qubole. Is that something you spend a lot of time thinking about?*

Ashish: Qubole has been data-driven from day one, so we spend a lot of...If you look at our typical internal meetings and stuff like that, if ever there's any issue being discussed, we always talk about data to back those issues. Whether it is bottlenecks and our business processes or bottlenecks anywhere, and so on and so forth, we always talk about data. Data has become very central at Qubole and it's been like that from day one. It's a truly data-driven company. We [inaudible 00:21:54] whatever we build. Whatever we build, we basically use that to analyze a lot of our product data, a lot of how people are using Qubole themselves. A lot of that data feeds into other business processes as well and we try to [inaudible 00:22:08] all of what we build and sort of practice what we preach. As a result, the company has been data-driven from day one.

Jon: *We've known a great deal about the power of data. For some time, the idea of using data to make decisions is not new among management experts and sort of IT technologists, but it seems that it's gotten a lot easier recently and I take it as it's connected to the cloud. I wonder if you could talk about how the cloud has changed the way that it's possible to build a data-driven culture.*

Ashish: That's true. Cloud had a huge effect in accelerating this transformation of making companies data-driven and making that type of culture accessible, that type of culture and technology accessible to a large set of companies than just companies like Facebook or the Google AdWords. How does a cloud help here? There are two [inaudible 00:23:05] reasons.

First, cloud is built on self-service principles. If you look at whether it is the first wave of cloud computing or the second wave of cloud computing, it is all built on making things as service, making it self-service. We have sort of also embraced that and cloud naturally leads to that type of interface for users to make it a self-service.

Now, the other critical thing is that once you make interface a self-service, you also have to back it up with infrastructure that is adaptable, that is flexible, that can scale up or scale down depending upon usage, that is automated because if you don't have that, then you are essentially again going back to a world where you are held prisoner to the capacity of data infrastructure and essentially you are limited by that. Cloud helps there as well because, again, the API automation of converting infrastructure into an API, allows you for the first time to react to these transformations and queries that are coming to the self-service interface and create infrastructure on the fly.

If you put these things together, you get a self-service platform and you get a self-managing and automated platform. As a result, what happens is that the companies don't have to invest in huge operational teams around us and at the same time, they get a platform. They also don't have to invest an integration on multiple tools to make it self-service. Therefore, all those things make it much easier for the companies to be able to get to a cutting-edge platform and they don't have to be a Facebook or a Google to do that anymore. Cloud has basically played that role for us and Qubole has been built on that thesis and essentially has embraced that. That is how we are bringing that same transformational benefits to self-service data infrastructure that had such a profound effect on companies like Facebook and Google AdWords. We are bringing that to all the other companies, to the mainstream companies as well, and our hope is that in that way, we can help user cloud to help drive the data-driven culture a lot in these companies.

Jon: *As with so many things, the cloud has democratized a kind of sophisticated intelligence and now it's possible for anyone to implement ... You don't have to invest billions of dollars in infrastructure to do it. You don't need to hire tens or hundreds of PhD-level researchers to do it. It's available as a service and easy to just sort of switch on.*

Ashish: That's correct. That is correct. That's absolutely correct.

Jon: *Terrific. Ashish Thusoo, thank you so much for joining me from Qubole. If the listeners would like to find you online, where should they look?*

Ashish: We are at *www.Qubole.com*, and I am on LinkedIn, Ashish Thusoo is my LinkedIn stub, and just send us an email or contact us at LinkedIn, and I will be happy to chat about this transformation.

Jon: *Terrific. Thank you so much.*

Ashish: Thank you, Jon.

About the Authors

Ashish Thusoo and **Joydeep Sen Sarma** were part of building and leading the original Facebook Data Service Team from 2007–2011 during which they authored many prominent data industry tools, including the Apache Hive Project. Their goal was not only to enable massive speed and scale to the data platform, but also to provide better self-service access to the data for business users. With the lessons learned from successes at Facebook, Qubole was launched in 2013 with these very same product principles: speed, scale, and accessibility in analytics. The company is headquartered in Santa Clara, CA, with offices in Bangalore, India.

CPSIA information can be obtained
at www.ICGtesting.com
Printed in the USA
FSOW04n1632310717
36870FS